P9-DNA-039

Praise for *The Grace Effect*

"Larry Taunton's book is a captivating account of a grim reality with a truly gracious ending. It is a must read for anyone pondering adoption from the former Eastern European Bloc. As such, *The Grace Effect* is a primer in applied Christianity that conveys a riveting, harrowing story of a child's hope quietly sustained by what psychologists increasingly recognize as a pervasive human capacity for spirituality. What the author uniquely achieves is to demonstrate the resilience of such a capacity even under some of the most unfavorable conditions at the start of life and, in this case, engulfing a wider society. Through the unfolding story of Sasha's life before and after adoption, Taunton skillfully weaves into the discussion about the meaning of human life some sobering contrasts between religious faith and strident atheism. This highly readable book is a collection of powerful insights into some of the long-term consequences of spiritual indifference and, above all, a remarkable example of how to conquer it."

— OLIVERA PETROVICH
*Research Psychologist, University
of Oxford.*

"*The Grace Effect—How the Power of One Life Can Reverse the Corruption of Unbelief* offers an ordinary story turned powerful narrative with a life-changing message. It is remarkable."

— ESTHER CALLENS
The Birmingham Times

"What would a world without Christianity look like? We don't have to guess because such a world *does* exist: it exists in the current and former Communist bloc. Through the inspiring story of a little girl born in Eastern Europe and now living in America, Larry Taunton draws a sharp contrast between the life-giving influence of Christianity and the worn out theories of atheism and radical secularism. The effect—*The Grace Effect*—is nothing less than powerful and moving."

— DINESH D'SOUZA
former White House policy
analyst, fellow of the Hoover
Institute at Stanford University,
and current president of Kings
College

The GRACE EFFECT

The GRACE EFFECT

How the Power of
One Life Can Reverse
the Corruption
of Unbelief

BY LARRY ALEX TAUNTON

THOMAS NELSON
Since 1798

NASHVILLE   DALLAS   MEXICO CITY   RIO DE JANEIRO

Published in Nashville, Tennessee, by Thomas Nelson. Thomas Nelson is a registered trademark of Thomas Nelson, Inc.

What Have We Become, written by Mark Heimermann, Toby Mckeehan, and Kevin Smith. © 1995 Blind Thief Publishing (BMI) Achtober Songs (BMI) Up in the Mix Music (BMI) (adm. at EMICMGPublishing.com) / Fun Attic Music (ASCAP). All rights reserved. Used by permission.

Unless otherwise indicated, Scripture quotations are taken from THE ENGLISH STANDARD VERSION. © 2001 by Crossway Bibles, a division of Good News Publishers.

Scriptures marked NIV are taken from the HOLY BIBLE: NEW INTERNATIONAL VERSION®. © 1973, 1978, 1984 by International Bible Society. Used by permission of Zondervan Publishing House. All rights reserved.

Thomas Nelson, Inc., titles may be purchased in bulk for educational, business, fund-raising, or sales promotional use. For information, please e-mail SpecialMarkets@ThomasNelson.com.

Library of Congress Cataloging-in-Publication Data

Taunton, Larry.
   The grace effect : how the power of one life can reverse the corruption of unbelief / by Larry Alex Taunton.
      p. cm.
   ISBN 978-1-59555-440-6 (alk. paper)
   1. Apologetics. 2. Christianity and atheism. 3. Taunton, Larry—Family. 4. Intercountry adoption—Ukraine. 5. Intercountry adoption—United States. I. Title.
   BT1212.T38 2011
   261.8'35874—dc22
   [B]   2011015265

Printed in the United States of America

11 12 13 14 15 QG 5 4 3 2 1

For Sasha and her mother, Lauri

What in me is dark, illumine,
What is low, raise and support;
That to the height of this great Argument
I may assert the Eternal Providence,
And justify the ways of God to men.

—John Milton's *Paradise Lost*

Contents

Contents

Preface

IN THE LAST DECADE, A GROUP OF PROMINENT ACADEMIC ATHEISTS has managed to channel a simmering anti-Christian fervor into a movement that seeks nothing less than a radical overhaul of Western civilization. Christianity, they say, is not only an outdated cultural accessory; it is also an insidious evil that we would be well-advised to discard. If my only knowledge of these men derived from the screeds they have written, it would be difficult to take them seriously. Unfortunately, many others, mostly the young and naive, have taken them seriously. Were it only a passing fashion like, say, rebellion against the establishment, I would be less inclined to worry about what all of this might portend for our society. But secularism is the establishment in Western society, and with the accumulated momentum of its century-long advance, we dare not take that chance.

Ironically, these revolutionaries—these so-called New

Atheists—really believe that they are doing us all a favor. Like bloodletters from centuries past, they think they are curing the patient, when they are in fact only making him more vulnerable to infection. May this book serve to remind us all just how diseased the body politic can become in the absence of Christian influence.

A word about what this book is not. It is not an effort to prove the existence of God. While I briefly address that issue, I am hunting game of an altogether different sort. I also have no desire to defend "religion" as such. My defense is limited to Christianity. What interest does a Christian have in defending suicide bombing and Sharia law? To this extent the New Atheists are right: some religions *are* irrational. Indeed, from a Christian perspective, all that do not lead to Jesus Christ are dead ends. Furthermore, this is not an academic work. There are enough of those already, and I saw no need to add to that still-growing pile. Instead, I have written with the layperson in mind.

It is, rather, my purpose to make a case for society's need of Christianity's gentling, inspiring, and culturally transforming power. I hope that through the narrative of our experience, readers will be given a glimpse into a world without faith in Jesus Christ and, as a consequence, have greater appreciation for what Christianity has given, is giving, and may give us still if we will mine the vast richness of it.

The Debate Begins

*It is in Christianity that our arts have developed;
it is in Christianity that the laws of Europe—
until recently—have been rooted. It is against a
background of Christianity that all of our thought
has significance. An individual European may
not believe that the Christian faith is true, and
yet what he says, and makes, and does will all
spring out of his heritage of Christian culture and
depend upon that culture for its meaning . . . I do
not believe the culture of Europe could survive the
complete disappearance of the Christian faith. And
I am convinced of that, not merely because I am a
Christian myself, but as a student of social biology.
If Christianity goes, the whole culture goes.*

—T. S. Eliot, *Christianity and Culture*[1]

IT WAS LATE. PAST MIDNIGHT, IN FACT, AND I WAS BLEARY-EYED.
Other diners had long since vacated the restaurant, and the
poor waiter hovered impatiently. As the executive director

1

of Fixed Point Foundation, an initiative dedicated to defending and promoting Christianity in the public square, I had
engaged numerous critics of that faith, and now, sitting
across the table from me was one of the most vitriolic—
famed atheist provocateur Christopher Hitchens. Also
present was University of Oxford mathematician Professor
John Lennox, a silver-tongued Irishman and Christian whom
I deeply admired. A few hours earlier, the two had debated
before a packed house at Samford University in Birmingham,
Alabama, on the question of whether belief in the Christian
God is beneficial or detrimental to society. Now, over dinner, the debate continued. Although an informal and friendly
exchange, we had been at it since ten o'clock.

"Christopher, whether Hitler had any authentic religious convictions or not—and I by no means concede that
he did—is irrelevant because he clearly was not motivated
by them," I argued. "He was motivated by a *Darwinian*
worldview."*

Hitchens had been trying to rid the atheist member-
ship roll of Hitler all night, first, during his debate with
Lennox, and now, with me. He said something about the

---

* In *Hitler: A Study in Tyranny*, historian Alan Bullock writes, "In Hitler's eyes
Christianity was a religion fit only for slaves; he detested its ethics in particular. Its
teaching, he declared, was a rebellion against the natural law of selection by struggle
and the survival of the fittest. . . . He was a rationalist and a materialist, with no
feeling or understanding for either the spiritual side of human life or its emotional,
affective side" (New York: HarperPerennial, 1991, 219). See also David Bentley Hart's
Atheist Delusions: The Christian Revolution and Its Fashionable Enemies (Yale
University Press, 2009), p. 14.

Catholic Church and its complicity with the Nazis during World War II as he signaled for another Johnnie Walker Black Label. The waiter, less cordial than when our dinner started some two hours ago, gave an exasperated look to no one in particular and practically jogged to the bar, no doubt driven more by a desire to hurry things along than to provide snappy service.

If all you know about Christopher Hitchens is the title of his best-selling book, *God Is Not Great: How Religion Poisons Everything*, then you will know that it is his assertion, like all aggressive secularists, that the world would be a better place without religion in general and without Christianity in particular. One of the self-proclaimed "Four Horsemen of the Counter-Apocalypse," he is—along with Richard Dawkins, Daniel Dennett, and Sam Harris—one of the "New Atheists," a group of best-selling authors dedicated to the eradication of religion from civilized society.

"Fascism," Hitchens asserted, "is synonymous with right-wing Catholicism, and was responsible for—"

Sometimes these discussions can degenerate into a body count. The atheist will say, "Christians were responsible for the Crusades, the Inquisition, and the Salem witch trials." The Christian will counter, "Atheists were responsible for Stalin, Hitler, Mao, and Pol Pot." The reasoning is not sound, and this particular conversation seemed headed in that direction. Before it got to that point, I asked, "In your view, is man intrinsically good or bad?"

His reply was as surprising as it was emphatic: "Man is unquestionably *evil*."

Hitchens, whose voice is reminiscent of Richard Burton, lent the last two syllables the full measure of his sonorous English baritone—"*Eee-vil*."

I had deliberately avoided that word in my question, as I assumed he would reject it as so much loaded dice. A week earlier in Beirut, however, neo-Nazis had attacked Hitchens and tried to bungle him into the back of a car after he defaced one of their posters, a bold move that nearly cost him his life. His countenance still bore the memory of it. Whatever his view of man before, it was decidedly cynical now.

Still, I was surprised. I had put this same question to other atheists, and he was the first to answer without some prevarication. His answer was, as he well knew, inconsistent with atheism, because in that world good and evil cease to exist. There is only what happens, but no moral judgments can be assigned to anything, as there are no absolute standards.

"Then it seems to me," I pressed, "that the question is this: which philosophies or religions restrain our darker impulses, and which ones *exacerbate* them?"

The waiter, cleaning a nearby table for the third time, was listening now. So was Hitchens. He appeared to be considering the question thoughtfully.

"Let me be more specific. Of our two worldviews"—I

gestured first at him and then at myself—"which one best addresses the problem of evil?"

"You think *religion* addresses it?" Hitchens asked with raised eyebrows. He then cited a litany of horrors done in the name of religion in the Middle East.

"No, not religion, Christopher," Lennox corrected in his disarming Irish manner. "*Christianity*. There is a difference." Having spent the first part of the evening publicly arguing the Christian position, Lennox now contented himself with points of clarification.

"And Christianity," I continued, picking up the thread, "begins with the premise that man is evil and that he needs to be saved from himself. Atheism, on the other hand, offers no compelling reason why I should not do precisely as I want to do." Hitchens gave a nod of agreement.

Since Christopher Hitchens is a friend of mine, I have had many conversations of this type with him, both in America and in the United Kingdom, and can tell you that he is a clever and articulate man. But even his formidable (and often ill-employed) powers of intellect and oratory seem rather vapid on this point. However, he must be forgiven for the deficiency. A godless worldview offers no meaningful answer to the question.

I had once asked this question of Richard Dawkins in his home in Oxford, England. Given the moral tenor of his antireligious crusading, this seemed a valid query. Predictably, Dawkins deemed notions of good and evil to be mere artificial human constructs, opting instead to speak of "genetic predispositions." Hitchens, however, was different. He needed no convincing of man's evil nature. An accomplished journalist, he had borne witness to human depravity all over the world. It had not left him unchanged. And if he is not the most credentialed of the New Atheists—he possesses no doctorates and is not a member of any royal societies—he is, nonetheless, the most broadly educated and intellectually honest. Yet even as Hitchens conceded my point on human nature, he remained no less skeptical of the idea that Christianity was the magic bullet.

"Larry, I think the history of Eastern Europe and the Orthodox Church in the twentieth century contradicts your thesis, does it not?" In addition to Hitler, the New Atheists have, against all logic and evidence to the contrary, tried to attribute the atrocities of Stalin and his heirs to Christianity, or, at the very least, to say that they have nothing to do with atheism.*

"Not at all," I replied emphatically. "Those were atheistic regimes that hijacked man's innate religious sentiment and gave him the state as his object of worship rather than God." Hitch looked dubious.

---

* In his book *The God Delusion*, Richard Dawkins argues that while Stalin was an atheist, there is no evidence that atheism was the motive for his crimes. It is an absurd point. Whatever Stalin's motivation—bitter jealousy, rivalry, hatred for his fellow man, or power—the evils he committed were surely *products* of his atheism. No one does anything for the sake of atheism, as though it were an entity to be appeased. Indeed, atheism has no creed, no principles, no philosophy, and can give no guidance. It is but to have a settled disposition on a single question: *Is there a God?* From that, however, many dominoes can, and often do, fall.

The conversation took a momentary detour as he related what were probably very real abuses committed by elements of the Russian Orthodox Church.*

Lennox, who has lectured and traveled extensively in Eastern Europe—both before and after the collapse of the Soviet Union—challenged the purpose if not the validity of these vignettes.

"Christopher, do you *really* think that you are undermining our position with references to stuff like that?" Lennox asked incredulously. "I don't doubt that the stories are true. I could add more stories of my own to the ones you have told! But they are not the actions of genuine *Christians*."

"You don't consider the Orthodox Church Christian?" Hitchens seemed confident in the response he would get.

"Well, it's not about this or that denomination or what we consider Christian or not Christian," I began slowly, looking at Lennox. "It's really a question of 'what does the Bible say?'"

At this, Hitchens sat up, totally astonished. Apparently, this was not the answer he expected. He turned to Lennox and gestured at me. "Do you agree with that, Professor?"

"I do," Lennox declared. "Christ forbad the very actions

---

* The actions of the Russian Orthodox Church during the Soviet period should not be attributed to Russian Orthodoxy. In 1937 alone, the NKVD executed some eighty-five thousand Orthodox priests while others languished in the Gulag. Those who remained were intimidated into cooperation with the regime. The Russian Orthodox Church had, in other words, been hijacked. Sovietologist Robert Conquest says that a "vicious and dogmatic atheism" characterized Soviet policy (*Stalin: Breaker of Nations* [New York: Penguin, 1992], 157). Religion had nothing whatsoever to do with the horrors of Stalinism.

you are calling 'Christian'!" The word *forbad*, evocative of early English translations of the Bible and spoken as it was, with an Irish accent, caused me to briefly imagine Saint Patrick thundering from a pulpit long ago. "Christ was even *more* resolute in his opposition to hypocrisy, exploitation, and the use of violence to promote his message than you are, Christopher." Lennox reached for his water glass, but it was empty. "Perhaps you should be one of his followers?" he added, putting the glass down.

This last bit was playful, and Hitchens received it in that manner, though he appeared to be processing what was manifestly a new definition of Christianity for him. The idea of the Bible as sole arbiter of what distinguishes authentic Christianity from counterfeit versions of it, a concept as old as Christianity itself, left him dumbfounded.

There was, for the first time, a pause in the conversation. Collecting my thoughts, I tried to come back to the central question—"One of my boys was just reading *The Lord of the Flies*. Do you remember the novel?"

"Of course. William Golding's classic." Hitchens, who has a deep appreciation for literature, probably knew it well.

"I didn't, really," I confessed. "So I decided to reread it. In doing so, I was reminded *why* it is a classic."

Hitchens slammed back what remained of his scotch and crossed his arms on the table, apparently interested in where I was going with this train of thought.

"I then became curious about Golding and read an interview where he said that the purpose of the book was to demonstrate that the problems of human society are the problems of human nature.[2] I don't know what Golding's religious beliefs were, but that is a profound point—"

"No doubt. He was an Oxford man," Hitchens, also an Oxford man, observed proudly.

"—and it is a profoundly *Christian* point," I said. At this, Hitchens's face registered what I took to be regret for having agreed with me. Somewhat amused, I proceeded.

"Now, you—that is, the 'New Atheists'—you want to—"

"You do realize that the term 'New Atheist' is not ours, don't you?" Hitchens interjected. "It was given to us by a journalist, I think."

"Yes, I realize that—"

"Glad to hear it, Christopher," Lennox quipped mischievously, "as I find little by way of innovation on the old atheism."

Hitchens regarded Lennox for a moment with a smile and then turned back to me. "You were saying?"

"Uh, yes. You," I continued, "the 'New Atheists' or 'Four Horsemen of the Counter-Apocalypse' or whatever you want to call yourselves, you say that the problem is *religion*. But you have as much as admitted during the course of this conversation that the problem is *not* religion. It is *man*. A religion, like, say, radical Islam, might exacerbate man's nature, but it is not responsible for it."

Now Lennox was the one raising his eyebrows. He watched Hitchens for a reaction. The latter seemed to be retracing his steps.

Knowing that he recognized the contradictory nature of his own argument, I sought to drive the point home. "Christianity, on the other hand, not only understands that the problem is man, but it seeks to redeem him from the evil that is inherent to his nature. It understands man's need for meaning, for love, and for hope, and it gives to society what it otherwise lacks—"

Hitch pursed his lips. "Well, I will certainly agree that Christianity once inspired great art and literature, but it is a relic of Bronze Age mythology—"

"No, I mean much more than art and literature," I said, ignoring the Bronze Age nonsense. "Christianity isn't just some kind of cultural accessory, working on the periphery of society, that we can discard without consequence. It has provided the foundation for society—"

"What? You mean that Christianity has given us tel-evangelists fleecing the unsuspecting? And parents teaching children to believe in a God who spies on them and will send them to hell if they do not do his bidding?" Hitchens put in sarcastically. But the remark lacked the force of previous occasions when I had heard it.

"That's not Christianity you're talking about." Lennox had heard these arguments from Hitchens before too.

"And it's certainly not what I'm talking about," I said dismissively. The conversation was very serious now, as though everyone sensed that we were finally at the heart of the issue.

"I am referring to what theologians call 'common grace,'" I explained. "It's the idea that when there is a significant

Christian presence in a given society, it brings tangible benefits not just to the Christian, but to society as a whole."

Hitchens seemed intrigued, if not fully convinced. He listened to these words with a seriousness to match that with which I had spoken them. What he was thinking, I cannot know, but it had always seemed to me that grace was the very thing atheists did not—perhaps could not—understand. Instead of a merciful, gracious God, they saw only the Rule of Saint Benedict on a cosmic scale.

"Hitch, you are evidence of it!" I declared. "You were educated at a university founded by Christians, believe in a science discovered by Christians, and draw many of your moral sensibilities from a Judeo-Christian tradition!" I decided to challenge him. "You know, I would love to study a book of the Bible with you sometime, say, the gospel of John?"

Hitchens raised an eyebrow and grinned. "You mean a mutual 'textual criticism'?"

"Yes, something like that. I don't think you've ever really read the Bible."

He nodded. "Agreed. I shall look forward to it."

IT WAS NOW ALMOST 1:00 A.M., AND HITCHENS WANTED ME TO take him to see the Sixteenth Street Baptist Church, the site of the infamous bombing that killed four little girls in 1963 during the civil rights movement.

Exhausted, I was hoping that the lateness of the hour

would dissuade him, but it did not. Lennox, in no mood for late-night adventures, sensibly bid us a good evening.

As I drove us to the church that is now a landmark, Hitch turned on the overhead light and put on his reading glasses, hoping to make sense of the lousy directions given to us at the restaurant. A few wrong turns later, he had me in front of the church. Pulling to the curb, he got out, left the door open, and read aloud the inscription on the large stone monument commemorating the tragedy. In that moment, the church and the monument seemed an unexpected metaphor for that evening's discussion. Here was a tangible example of evil defeated by a people who were motivated by a Christian conscience.

Getting back into the car, Hitchens was ready to respond to my earlier assertion that he was a beneficiary of certain Christian traditions. He knew that this much was true. But that did not, in his mind, prove that we had further need of Christianity. What does Christianity give us now? he asked. Yes, it has given us science and universities. Yes, it has given us great art and literature. But that was a long time ago, and we can get along very well without it.

By the time we arrived at my home, I could see that the idea of Christianity as a positive contributor to society seemed too remote in history for the full weight of my meaning to be felt. It was as though I were arguing for the greatness of the Classical Greeks. Sure, they gave us something valuable, but having given it, the Greeks were themselves superfluous. What are the modern benefits of a Christian presence in society? *Where is common grace to be found now?* As Hitchens retired to our guest room for the night, the matter remained unresolved. What I didn't then know was that I was about to discover the meaning of common grace by entering a world where there was an absence of it.

Note: After writing this account of our conversation, I presented it to John and Christopher for their approval. I did so for two reasons: first, I did not want to publish anything that was deemed private; second, I wanted to submit my recollections of the evening to their scrutiny. Both say that this is an accurate account of our discussion, although Hitchens did correct one thing: his drink of choice. I originally had him drinking Johnnie Walker Red Label.

ONE

First Steps

*The White Rabbit put on his spectacles. "Where
shall I begin, please your Majesty?" he asked.
"Begin at the beginning," the King said gravely,
"and go on til you come to the end: then stop."*

—FROM LEWIS CARROLL'S *ALICE IN WONDERLAND*

WE SAT IN MEMPHIS INTERNATIONAL AIRPORT, WAITING TO
board our flight. My wife, Lauri, passed the time talking
to friends on her cell phone while it was still possible to
do so. A few seats away, Christopher, our sixteen-year-old
son, was oblivious to the cacophony of voices, rolling luggage, and loudspeakers that are common to such settings.
An avid reader, he was deep into Huxley's *Brave New World.*
Zachary, the youngest of our brood, fidgeted restlessly and
then, as though divinely inspired, looked at me hopefully.

"Hey, Daddy-o? How about some barbecue before we
leave the country?" At thirteen, he wasn't much for either
cell phone chitchat or Huxley's secular prophecies. He and
our other boys had affectionately called me "Daddy-o" ever

since giving me the screen name "Daddy-07" in one of their James Bond video games years before.

"Sure," I said, checking my watch. A Southerner both in heart and palate, it required little to persuade me to eat barbecue at any time. Christopher's audio-sensory filters, which worked to prevent anything he deemed inconsequential from reaching his conscious being while reading, had certain preset exceptions. All of them dealt with food.

"Barbecue?" he said, perking up. "Did someone say 'barbecue'?" A few minutes and a trip to an airport kiosk later, we sat eating our pork sandwiches, wondering what we would find ahead of us in the coming days.

Our family—minus our oldest son, Michael, who was then in college—was traveling to Ukraine to finalize the adoption of a ten-year-old girl named Sasha. Waiting for our flight, Christopher and Zachary saw it all as a great adventure. They had met Sasha the previous summer while on a short-term mission trip to Odessa. In fact, the whole family had met her but me. The work in the orphanage had made an enormous impression on all of them, and now, almost a year later, I was going with them to adopt the little girl they knew and of whom I had only heard stories and seen pictures.

"Ladies and gentlemen, we will continue boarding with our passengers traveling in business elite . . ."

Business elite. Definitely not us. Boarding for our zone, which lay about a football field from business elite, wouldn't take place for another fifteen minutes or so. Nevertheless, the boys and I wolfed down what remained of our sandwiches while Lauri scurried to gather the carry-on luggage. Efficiency is part of an American's DNA.

"How long do you think we will be gone?" Lauri asked as we joined a growing line of passengers. It was as if she were seeking my prediction on the outcome of a sporting event.

"Hmmm . . ." I tried to take all of the variables into account. "I'll say four weeks."

"We will continue boarding with our passengers seated in Zone 1."

Lauri looked hopeful but uncertain about my prediction. I was confident that we would be able to expedite the process once in Ukraine. A friendly conversation with the right Ukrainian official might help them see that it was in everyone's best interest to move things along. Sasha, a special-needs child, would greatly benefit from better health care, and to leave her in an orphanage even a day longer than was necessary seemed cruel, especially since she had been waiting a lifetime.

Over the years, Lauri and I had often discussed adoption, but something always prevented us from doing it. Now it was going to happen, and we were excited that a year-long process was approaching an end. Viewed from the perspective of my work, however, this presented some difficulties. Adoptive parents spend an average of thirty-six days in Ukraine, and we were told to expect nothing different. I felt that I could scarcely afford that much time away. Furthermore, we had no control over the timing of our trip. Once the appropriate documents for adoption were submitted to the Ukrainian government, parents waited to be issued travel dates, and those are immovable—or, more accurately, the government won't move them. A refusal to appear when summoned is to risk the adoption altogether. One can imagine how this wreaks havoc on schedules. Hence, it became a contentious point.

"Can't you just go over there and get her?" I would ask Lauri. "The Ukrainians want us to come when I am supposed to be in China."

"No, dear, you have to be there too," Lauri would remind me.

"Brad and Sue adopted from Eastern Europe, and *he* didn't have to go."

"Brad and Sue adopted from *Bulgaria*. The laws are different in Ukraine."

"Next time, let's adopt from Bulgaria," I said, defeated and not planning on a next time. We'd had this conversation before, and the result was always the same. Frustrated, I looked for some way to follow through with the adoption while not abandoning my work. Reluctantly, I resigned myself to the fact that I would have to go. I canceled the China trip, postponed engagements where it was possible to do so, and delegated what remained of my calendar. And as Lauri pointed out, since I would be free from the daily distractions of meetings and phone calls, I might find that I was able to accomplish a great deal in Ukraine. Multitasking, however, does not come natural to me, and doing such disparate things as fulfilling my professional responsibilities while daily seeing to the personal ones associated with this adoption some eight time zones away did not give me much reason for optimism. The two were, in my mind, utterly unrelated.

Cruising some 35,000 feet over the Eastern Seaboard, we settled in for the transatlantic flight.

"So, how are you enjoying your book, Christopher?" I had reread Huxley only a few weeks before and urged my children to read him too.

"It's pretty good." He looked up, holding his page with a finger. Zachary sat between us, playing an electronic game and wearing headphones.

"Yeah, that's why they call it a 'classic,'" I said with a smile, trying to draw out his opinion. "Can you tell me more?"

Chris looked up at the luggage compartment for a moment, gathering his thoughts.

"Well, it's not what I expected," he began. "I mean, I know that Huxley was an atheist, but so far—I'm only half-way through the book—it doesn't seem like he thinks a world without belief in God would be a very good thing."

"That's a perceptive analysis."

It doesn't seem like he thinks a world without belief in God would be a very good thing. Involuntarily, the conversation with Christopher Hitchens in the restaurant a fortnight before replayed in my mind. How does one quantify common grace?

At this point, it is probably important that I explain what I mean by "common grace." That God grants both temporal and eternal blessings to the Christian is—among Christians, anyway—axiomatic. My faith in Jesus Christ not only gives me hope through the forgiveness of my sins and the promise of eternal life, but also, through the work of the Holy Spirit, offers me guidance in the daily discharge of my affairs. When Christians speak of grace, this is usually what they mean, and while true, this does not mark the outer boundary of God's gracious activity. Common grace should not be confused with "saving" or "special" grace, which is a very different doctrine. One theologian defined common grace as that grace which "curbs the destructive power of sin, maintains in a measure the moral order of the universe, thus making an orderly life possible, distributes in varying degrees gifts and talents among men, promotes the development of science and art, and showers untold blessings upon the children of men."[1] This is a rather theologian-like way of saying that common grace is that grace which may be enjoyed by believers as well as unbelievers, though the former understand its source. And it is grace because it is divinely given and undeserved by the recipient. It was this doctrine that the apostle Paul had in mind when he wrote that God "is the savior of all people, especially of those who believe" (1 Timothy 4:10).

So, practically speaking, how does God achieve this? First, he does it by sustaining the natural order. The author of Hebrews wrote, "He upholds the universe by the word of his power" (1:3). In his address to the Athenians, Paul brought this concept down to earthly proportions, saying, "[God] gives to all mankind life and breath and everything" (Acts 17:25). In other words, that the universe does not explode like the Death Star is due to God's providential mercy. And clearly that is of benefit to more than just Christians.

God also blesses mankind by restraining our evil nature. We are told that God has written his law upon the hearts of men (Romans 2:15). This law finds expression in the conscience. Conscience may compel us to help someone in need or to seek forgiveness from those we have wronged, or it may lead us to the Cross itself. Conscience is the soul's voice. When contravened, it cries out.

Of course, conscience can be killed, according to 1 Timothy 4:2. Just as speed bumps on a road serve to warn drivers, so conscience works, jostling us from a moral slumber. Violated often enough, however, its voice grows fainter. When that happens and human nature is left to indulge its evil appetites, we become "filled with all manner of unrighteousness, evil, covetousness, malice" (Romans 1:29). Thankfully, God further restrains humanity through government institutions, which are, in effect, a collective conscience (see Romans 13:1–7). And when those fail, Auschwitzes and Darfurs are the result.

But there is another form that common grace assumes, and it finds greatest expression in those cultures where Christianity has significantly influenced the public mind. In 1 Corinthians 7, the apostle Paul tells us that in a marriage where one spouse is a Christian and the other is not, the unbelieving member of that union is "made holy" through interaction with his or her believing husband or wife (v. 14). The presence of a Christian in the relationship not only serves to restrain the conduct of the unbeliever; it prepares him or her for a relationship with Jesus Christ.

This principle has implications that go well beyond marriage. Applying it to society as a whole, we begin to understand how common grace works. Here, common grace does much more than negate the evil impulses of mankind; it is a positive force for good. As one experiences grace in his own life, he extends grace to others. Through the inward transformation of the individual, there is a corresponding outward transformation of society. This is what I call the "grace effect." Simply defined, it is an observable phenomenon—*that life is demonstrably better where authentic Christianity flourishes.* Perhaps all of this seems too theoretical. At this point, it did to me, too.

TWO

Reality Check

"Toto, . . . we're not in Kansas anymore."

—DOROTHY IN *THE WIZARD OF OZ*

AS WE DESCENDED THROUGH THE CLOUDS AND OVER THE patchwork countryside, Kiev's Boryspil International Airport came into view. I had been in Ukraine several times before and had always thought that the airport, austere and something of a shambles, looked typical of the Soviet era. Alighting on the tarmac, the sleek KLM Boeing appeared oddly out of place. Lauri and the boys, exhausted from the Birmingham-Memphis-Amsterdam-Kiev journey, boarded the bus to the terminal slowly. It was mid-March, and the air was crisp under a brooding sky. Bouncing toward our destination, people checked messages and made calls, but they remained remarkably quiet. Colorfully attired (by Ukrainian standards) and talkative (by any standard), we may have been the loudest on that bus but for a couple of middle-aged men with their much-younger female companions. Thick-necked, sporting buzz cuts and skintight shirts stretched over heavily muscled and tattooed frames, they looked like Ivan Drago clones. Curiously, this type is ubiquitous to the former East Bloc. Their women, however, were another story altogether. Weighted down with bags from fashionable clothing stores, they had apparently been taken to western Europe by their muscular escorts to do a bit of shopping. Having returned triumphantly, they displayed their spoils ostentatiously.

Passing through the gauntlet of passport control, baggage claim, and customs, we entered the central terminus and began scanning the crowd for our Ukrainian adoption facilitator, Ivan. Although he was unknown to us, we were told that he would be wielding a sign bearing our name: Taunton. We saw nothing of the sort. No matter. With each of us rolling a Samsonite and everything about us proclaiming "American," we were easily identifiable to him.

"Larry! How are you?" A stout, dark-haired man emerged from a veritable midway of barking taxi drivers and extended his hand to me in a vigorous shake. "Follow me."

Ivan, like almost every other man in Ukraine, wore a dark leather jacket and took little notice of obstacles, be they human or automotive. "How was your trip? Tiring, yes?" he said, looking back over his shoulder occasionally but not waiting for a reply. He smiled broadly as he navigated the chaotic parking lot.

"How did you—?" I began.

"I have your picture," he said, shouting over the din. "It was e-mailed to me."

"Oh . . ."

As we drove to the city center, he chatted affably about the weather, Russo-Ukrainian relations, and his experiences in America. "I love California," he declared, sounding oddly like Arnold Schwarzenegger in the process. For more than a decade, Ivan had been assisting foreigners in their adoption of Ukrainian children. Most of his clients were American, and their effect on him was noticeable. Ivan had developed a taste for more than the California sun. He had absorbed much American pop culture and was partial to American standards of living.

"So, what is first on the agenda?" I asked, noting a Led Zeppelin CD pressed between the seats.

Ivan checked his rearview mirror and then maneuvered the Czech-made Škoda into the right lane. "I will take you to your hotel and then pick you up tomorrow morning." A big Mercedes sedan accelerated past us. Eyeing it, he continued. "We will then go to the SDA [State Department of Adoption] and initiate the adoption."

"And then what?" Lauri, in the backseat, had anticipated my next question. Beside her, Chris and Zach shifted uncomfortably beneath the suitcases on their laps.

"And then, *if* everything goes well"—he shrugged—"you will travel to Odessa." The "if" was delivered in a way that only a Ukrainian (or a Russian) can manage and that we would become so accustomed to hearing. It is not a question of accent, but of mood. Where *if* suggests hopeful possibilities when an American employs it, the same English word conveys something like an anticipation of doom in Ukrainian usage.

Ivan gave me a sideways glance and then, after a moment's pause, began our orientation. The whole of his address may be summarized in a brief sentence: *Lower your expectations.* Before us lay a number of obstacles—trips to an assortment of government agencies in Kiev and Odessa; meetings with various government officials; a court appearance; passports and a visa—and if all went well, we might be able to leave the country in six weeks. It sounded like one of those exciting "adventure races" where people travel across the country, hitting various checkpoints, but one sponsored by the Department of Motor Vehicles and therefore neither adventurous nor much of a race, since time would mean nothing and the winners were all predetermined. I wondered how many times he had given this talk, demolishing whatever optimism new arrivals came with. Regardless, Ivan knew Ukrainian governmental inertia and American expectations of efficiency. The two were incompatible, and it was better to know it at the outset. It was a bit like getting off a bus, wearing a swimsuit and suntan lotion, and asking, "Where's the beach?" only to be told that you're in Iowa.

FACILITATORS ARE KEY TO ANY INTERNATIONAL ADOPTION, AND Ivan had come highly recommended. Natives of the country from which you are trying to adopt, the good ones—as Ivan would prove to be—understand much more than the language, local customs, and laws. In addition to providing translation of proceedings and documents, they liaise between prospective parents and government officials, with whom relationships are occasionally strained. By local standards, they are paid handsomely for their services, and because they work on behalf of their clients rather than the government, some resentment is inevitable.

After we were settled into our hotel, the boys and I headed out to explore the surrounding area. The narrow alleys, busy streets, convenience stores, coffee shops, and restaurants were like those of every major metropolitan center in Europe or America. Setting this landscape apart, however, was the skyline, dominated as it was by St. Michael's Golden-Domed Monastery. A walk through the monastery grounds along a grassy footpath splendidly shaded by birch trees presents first-time visitors with an unexpected delight. Standing at a precipice you see, far below you, the Dnieper River winding through the heart of Kiev.

Founded in the ninth century, Kiev is now a city of some 3 million people and is both the capital of Ukraine and its largest city. The medley of architectural styles serves as a metaphor for the nation's history—onion-domed cathedrals of the Byzantine style, with beautiful Venetian interiors; a neoclassic palace; a grand concert hall in the Gothic manner; Baroque churches with iconostases; and the concrete monstrosities of the Soviet period—it all speaks of a clash—schizophrenia, really—between East and West. Unfortunately, the past most visible to any visitor, and in more than just the architecture, is the Soviet one, as we would soon discover.

The next morning, we began what seemed like an endless tour of Ukrainian government buildings. As Ivan fought the morning traffic, he pointed out various landmarks along Khreshchatyk Street, Kiev's main thoroughfare, and told us what to expect at our meeting with the SDA. (Every Ukrainian adoption must go through the SDA the way it seems every Delta flight must go through Atlanta.) The purpose of the meeting, he told us, was to receive a "referral." This simply meant approval to be considered as adoptive parents for a specific child. We should answer any questions briefly and let him do the rest of the talking.

Arriving at the SDA, we entered through a heavy, solid-steel door—every building is fortified with them in anticipation, no doubt, of the next revolution—and joined those already gathered there. There was no lobby, no waiting room, and no seats. Instead, people stood in a small, dim stairwell, waiting to be called. Ivan pushed through those who blocked the steps to the second floor and made our presence known to the appropriate official. Taking a number, we waited.

Eventually, a young, heavyset woman, dressed in black (they all are) emerged from a hallway atop the stairwell and summoned us. Ivan gave a "here we go" kind of look and led us into her office. She invited us to sit down and produced a file.

"You wish to adopt?" Ivan said, translating her Russian. She looked at us expectantly.

"Yes, we do."

"It is our understanding that you wish to adopt Oleksandra [Sasha is to Alexandra, or Oleksandra, what Jack is to John]. Is this correct?" She read from the file in her lap, waited for Ivan's Russian-to-English translation, watched for our response, and then listened as Ivan translated our English into Russian. Chris and Zach sat silently.

"Yes, we do."

"Are you aware of the child's condition?" she asked in reference to Sasha's health. She watched us closely.

"Yes, we are."

"According to our file"—she thumbed through the pages of it—"in addition to her other illness, Oleksandra has been diagnosed with hydrocephalus and rickets." She paused to allow Ivan to catch up. "This is according to a doctor's report dated . . ." She scanned the document. "July 1999. At that time, the hydrocephalus was dismissed."

Lauri and I looked at each other but said nothing. *Sasha has rickets?* This was news we had not expected. The SDA woman followed our eyes.

"Do you still want to adopt Oleksandra?" Again, she studied us.

"Yes, we do."

She smiled graciously. "Bless you," she said with a spirit of genuine warmth and almost bouncing in her chair. Composing herself, she once again became very serious and proceeded to read from Sasha's file.

"Orphanage #17 is Oleksandra's third since she was abandoned at birth. Her biological mother's real identity is not known . . ." What followed was an avalanche of depressing and degrading information of this sort. Ivan translated rapidly. There was nothing positive, nothing that told us about the child herself, like "She is very outgoing, likes to play soccer and with Barbie dolls . . ." None of that. To hear it grieved us.

Finished with all that she was required to do, the SDA woman rose. "There is one more thing," she said quietly, hesitating for a moment. "The adoption inspector in Odessa may prove troublesome." At first, she spoke slowly, but then, perhaps to save time, she spoke directly to Ivan in a somewhat hurried manner. He nodded and asked a few questions, and then she opened her door and escorted us to the hall. Once again, she said, "Bless you," squeezing our hands, her face filled with emotion.

Stepping outside into a light rain, we heard the heavy steel door slam behind us.

"What did she say?" we asked with curiosity.

Ivan unlocked the doors to his Škoda with the remote; the lights flashed.

"She said that the adoption inspector in Odessa could require you to locate Sasha's birth mother to get her permission." This was the foreboding Ukrainian *if*-factor.

I was dumbfounded. "What? How do we do that?"

"She just told us that *they* don't even know the mother's name or whereabouts," Lauri added, feeling much as I did.

"That is not all." Ivan started the car. "If Sasha was not born in Odessa, she may also require you to travel to the city or town where she was born to find her birth certificate."

This made no sense. Hadn't they ever heard of FedEx?

Lauri looked angry. She leaned up between the front seats.

"Ivan, why would we need to find her birth mother?"

Ivan, who was used to being the bearer of bad news to Americans, seemed not the least bit surprised.

"Well, *legally* you don't," he declared matter-of-factly. "But the adoption inspector has the power to make you get the mother's approval to adopt Sasha."

A somber silence ensued.

Sasha's biological mother, who had not contacted Sasha since giving birth to her ten years before, had no known addresses or name. It wasn't even certain that she was alive. Back at our hotel, we tried to absorb what this would mean.

And then there was the unexpected information concerning Sasha's medical history. We knew that she was a special-needs child, but the additional diagnosis of rickets had unsettled us. Rickets is a disease of poverty. It is a weakening of the bones due to a vitamin D deficiency, the result of malnutrition. I think Lauri and I both felt profoundly moved to hear this because, in addition to her other health challenges, it said a great deal about her overall care as an infant.

SAYING GOODBYE TO IVAN, WE DEPARTED KIEV EARLY THE NEXT morning, taking a twin-prop south to Odessa. As the flight attendant rattled off the usual safety instructions in

Ukrainian, Russian, and English, I looked out the window and wondered how much Sasha knew. Did she know we were coming for her? Would she remember Lauri and the boys? It had been almost a year since she had seen them. And how would she respond to me, a man whom she had never met?

Orphanage #17. The name sounded cold and institutional. For three years it had been Sasha's home. Before that, other orphanages with similarly cozy names. We hoped to change that.

THREE

Atheists Don't Do Benevolence

With respect to volunteer effort, two-thirds of
churchgoers give their time to non-profit causes
while only 43 percent of non-attendees do likewise.
And churchgoers put in twice as many hours
volunteering.

—*MACLEAN'S* MAGAZINE, MAY 6, 2010[1]

AMONG THE MANY THINGS FOR WHICH CHRISTOPHER HITCHENS has gained notoriety is a challenge he puts to his audiences or readers: "Name me an ethical statement made or an action performed by a believer that could not have been made or performed by a non-believer."[2] The idea is that there is no good thing that a Christian can do that an atheist cannot do also. At first blush, this challenge seems to have merit. An atheist can, for instance, perform works of charity and maintain high moral standards just as any Christian is supposed to do. But that is, as I have said, only at first blush, because the "challenge" is a sham. It's kind of like asking, "What can an herbivore eat that a carnivore cannot eat also?" After all, a hyena *can* eat grass, leaves, and bark just as an elephant does. But the fact is, hyenas *don't* eat grass, leaves, and bark, because it is not in their nature to do so.

Similarly, while atheists can perform works of charity or maintain high moral standards, history reveals that they *don't* with any degree of consistency. The statistics bear this out. According to a study conducted by the Barna Group, Christians are the most charitable segment of the population. The same study indicates that the average evangelical gives almost *ten times* as much money to nonprofits as the average atheist.[3]

This is not to say that there aren't some charitable and decent nonbelievers, or even some *un*charitable and *im*moral *believers*. Rather, when atheism is adopted as a worldview at a societal level, be it passively or actively, its effect on that society is detrimental. The point is beyond dispute. The greatest horrors the world has ever known have been perpetrated by *secular* regimes in the Soviet Union, China, Germany, North Korea, Cambodia, Vietnam—and the list goes on. In his book *The Devil's Delusion: Atheism and Its Scientific Pretensions*, David Berlinski makes the point brilliantly:

> What Hitler did *not* believe and what Stalin did *not* believe and what Mao did *not* believe and what the SS did *not* believe and what the Gestapo did *not* believe and what NKVD did *not* believe and what the commissars, functionaries, swaggering executioners, Nazi doctors, Communist Party theoreticians, intellectuals, Brown Shirts, Black Shirts,

gauleiters, and a thousand party hacks did *not* believe was that God was watching what they were doing. And as far as we can tell, very few of those carrying out the horrors of the twentieth century worried overmuch that God was watching what they were doing either.

That is, after all, the *meaning* of a secular society.*

Conversely, it has been Christian initiatives that have brought relief to many of the world's suffering through the building of schools, hospitals, shelters, homes, and, yes, churches; through short- and long-term missionary efforts; and through generous giving, thus making all of the afore-mentioned possible. Just a simple evaluation of efforts to relieve global epidemics of hunger, poverty, homelessness, and poor education reveals that it comes from the West, a culture heavily influenced by its lingering Christian memory, and of those countries, the United States most of all. It does not come from North Korea, China, or their ilk, regimes that are secularist (i.e., atheist by definition) to their black-hearted core. Hyenas don't do benevolence.

ODESSA, SOME 275 MILES SOUTH OF KIEV, SITS ON THE NORTHERN coast of the Black Sea. Looking eastward from the air, you can see its many ports reaching out into the water like

---

* (New York: Basic, 2009), 26–27; emphasis in original. David, a Jew, knows his subject. His parents fled Europe in the late '30s to avoid the Holocaust that became the fate of some of his extended family.

fingers, while all around and stretching into the horizon lie the gently undulating steppes upon which the city has been built. The little commuter flight unloaded quickly and in the smaller confines of Odessa International Airport, we had no trouble locating our new facilitator.

"Mr. Taunton?" he asked, as if embarrassed. "I am Viktor. I will be assisting you while you are here in Odessa."

A tall thirtysomething, he had blond, close-cropped hair and a friendly, inviting quality about him. Shaking my hand, he bowed ever so slightly and offered to help with our luggage. A native of Lviv in western Ukraine, he had only arrived in Odessa minutes before us, having traveled a full day by train. (A heroic feat, if you know anything about Ukrainian trains.)

Christopher and Zachary assisted the hotel's shuttle driver in piling our luggage into a van. Never smiling, speaking, or even stopping to flick the growing ash from the end of the cigarette that dangled from his thin lips, he just grunted as he lifted our suitcases that were packed to within an ounce of airline regulation limits.

"I have arranged for us to see the adoption inspector in one hour's time," Viktor informed us. "May I suggest that we go there immediately from the hotel?"

And so it was. We were now going to meet the woman we had been warned about in Kiev. Even her title sounded sinister: *adoption inspector*. (Or AI, as she would become known to us.) Since this was his first time in Odessa, Viktor did not know where her office was located. So, with map in hand, I navigated as he sent us careening down highway and boulevard as though we'd been shot from a cannon. I had no objection, but I think I could feel Lauri's fingernails digging into the back of the seat.

"No, no, turn right here," I nearly shouted over the loud humming of Viktor's little Mitsubishi.

"Here?" Viktor asked, gripping the steering wheel with both hands and following my pointing finger.

"Yes. Okay, good. Straight ahead . . ."

WE ARRIVED LATE, BUT SINCE YOU HAVE TO WAIT FOR EVERYTHING in Ukraine, it was probably inconsequential. The building was like almost any other government facility in the former East Bloc. Imagine a Khrushchev-era, bad neoclassic eyesore of the type that was then being thrown up all over the Soviet Union. (And I do mean *thrown up*.) Imagine a building that is in such a state of disrepair that you expect a wrecking ball to come smashing through a corridor at any moment or to feel charges being detonated beneath your feet, sending the whole thing collapsing in upon itself. Ceiling and floor tiles missing; bathrooms and stalls that appeared to have been designed with malice aforethought; and a hulking, formidable architecture meant to intimidate those who entered into passive obedience.

It was here that we met with the woman, the AI, whose reputation, title, and surroundings might have suggested that she was a SMERSH operative. Wearing a suit that appeared to be two sizes too small, she smiled at us through bad teeth and directed us to the chairs in front of her desk. Looking over her eyeglasses, she briefly inspected our file and appeared to chasten Viktor in stern tones. He stood somewhat anxiously beside her, bowing slightly, saying nothing. Then, as if noting our presence for the first time, she removed her spectacles and nibbled one of the temples while she silently considered us. Replacing them, she knitted her brow seriously and sat forward in her chair, leaning over the papers from our file, now spread across her desk. Speaking rapidly through Viktor, she fired away at me with a veritable barrage of questions, stopping occasionally to bark at our translator.

"What do you do?" she asked me, and "How much do you earn?" and "How many square meters is your house?" and so on. I was disconcerted by these unexpected questions. Fumbling with my smartphone, I tried to convert U.S. dollars into Ukrainian hryvnia and square feet into square meters. Of course, the answers to all of these questions were in the file she held. Lauri, trying to help, filled the silence with pleasantries while I thumbed my way to success. "How long have you worked here?" she asked, and "Is that a picture of your family?" But the AI wasn't the chatty sort.

Apparently satisfied with my responses, she then marched us to an adjacent office to meet her supervisor, an older woman whose precise function remains a mystery to us—we simply called her the "adoption inspector supervisor" (AIS). She reviewed our dossier in the same officious manner of her subordinate. Looking up from time to time, she questioned the AI, who now stood uncomfortably beside her. The student, it seems, had learned well from the master. The rest of us sat before the AIS in respectful silence.

It slowly dawned on me that Christopher and Zachary's presence was a matter of some interest to the AIS. The boys offered tangible evidence of what Lauri and I were like as parents. She observed them closely and smiled admiringly. They stood statue-erect, chins up, hands at their sides, like troops on review. Of course, only moments before they had probably been threatening to beat one another into unconsciousness, but the architecture had the desired effect on them—they were subdued, perhaps frightened. The AIS closed the file, and the meeting was over. She then gave a number of unintelligible (to non-Russian-speakers) commands, Viktor gave his obligatory bow, and we left.

"What was that all about?" I asked. Viktor gave a shrug.

"It is normal. She has given permission for you to go to the orphanage to meet the director and the child."

Back at the little Mitsubishi, a young, uniformed man joined us. Lauri and I exchanged puzzled glances. I speculated about his occupation: Police officer? Naval cadet? Inspector of adoption inspectors? Noting our bewilderment, Viktor pointed the man to a waiting taxi and then whispered to me, "The adoption inspector has sent him to supervise your meeting at the orphanage." Adoption meeting supervisor (AMS)? *Ding!*

LEAVING CENTRAL ODESSA, WE NOTED THAT THE TRAFFIC became sparser and the surroundings depressed. We followed the taxi in Viktor's car and twenty minutes later pulled up in front of a gated compound. Getting out of the car, I noted the grassless, largely treeless, indeed, almost lunar landscape and the bleak buildings that stood around the periphery of a courtyard. My boys had told me that the orphanage looked like an army barracks. *Perhaps in the Somali armed forces*, I thought, surveying what appeared to be an abandoned industrial site.

The AMS led us to the orphanage director's office. The director was a cheery, animated woman of about fifty. A buxom bleach blond, she wore red boots with thick, white laces tied just below the knee. Apparently delighted to see us, she greeted us enthusiastically and instructed her assistant to find Sasha.

"She is a happy girl!" she declared through our translator. "She has lots of energy and loves to play!" This was the sort of information that had been absent from the SDA records in Kiev. Data, I decided, is dehumanizing.

Through the office window that looked out onto the denuded quadrangle, Christopher spotted Sasha walking hand in hand with her teacher. Both were coming to the office.

"She sees us!" Zach observed excitedly.

Indeed, she had. She skipped ahead of her teacher and then broke into a full sprint, pausing occasionally, impatiently, for her teacher to catch up. Sasha burst into the office, immediately hugging Lauri, Christopher, and Zachary. She had not forgotten them.

"Michael?" she asked.

"He couldn't come," Lauri explained through Viktor. "He has school."

I was struck by Sasha's lively presence, her bouncing ponytail, and the fact that I could not understand a word she was saying. After greeting Lauri and the boys warmly, she acknowledged me with some reservation.

"How . . . ah . . . you?" she asked slowly and with a pronounced accent. This was clearly a phrase she had been practicing.

"I . . . am . . . fine," I replied slowly. "I am happy to finally meet you." Of course, she didn't understand, but it was a good start to our relationship.

The director encouraged Sasha to give us a tour of the dormitories. Out in the quadrangle, she once again skipped ahead, pausing from time to time to explain to other children who we were. We could not understand all of what she said, but Lauri and I both repeatedly heard "mama and papa." We were her parents, she told them proudly.

"She is also telling them that these are her brothers," Viktor added. She was confident in her surroundings. Strong willed and independent, she carried herself with a kind of strut, her ponytail flailing above her long strides. Her skills as a guide might have qualified her as one of London's finest. I could almost picture her saying, "To your right you will see the Houses of Parliament . . ."

One of life's tender mercies is found in not knowing how bad things really are. Ignorance, as they say, is bliss. Like so many aphorisms, this one surely overstates the case. But there is no doubt that dreadful circumstances are made more tolerable by having known nothing better. Of course, this wasn't London, and these crude buildings weren't the Houses of Parliament, but they were what typified the whole of Sasha's life. So if ignorance didn't constitute bliss, it did impart a measure of mercy.

Outside her dormitory, a junkyard dog barked as he strained against a heavy chain anchored to a concrete-filled tire. Children stood in corridors, staring at us. Some, recognizing Christopher and Zachary from the previous summer, greeted them excitedly. Taking my hand, Sasha led us inside, and there, in stark contrast with the dismal grounds, we saw walls painted or wallpapered in bright, cheerful colors; furniture and bunks in good repair; and in some rooms, carpet. One boy showed us his stuffed animals; another child, her storybooks; and yet another, his Frisbee. Make no mistake about it: the dorm was spartan, but it was not without some warmth.

These modest improvements, I discovered, were the work of American short-term missionaries, some of whom were from Covenant Presbyterian Church—our church in Birmingham, Alabama. These men and women took time from their families and work to travel around the world to help those who were less fortunate than themselves. And while I call them modest improvements, they were really

Photo by Christopher Taunton

The orphanage grounds.

a great deal more than that. It was the difference between meeting minimal physical needs and providing for those of the soul. I looked for any work that might have been done by atheist mission teams, but then it occurred to me that the whole diabolical orphanage system was their singular contribution to the misery that prevailed in these places.

Sasha, chattering in an endless stream of Russian, led us from room to room like captives before a Roman triumph. Opening a drawer, she produced the letters we had sent her. She introduced her friends—and even one or two with whom she appeared to be on less-cordial terms. That they all had been expecting us was clear. Children came from all over the orphanage to see us. Adoption was not so common that it had ceased to interest them. Gathering around, they pressed up against us. One little fellow clung to me with such ferocity that when I finally leaned over to put him down, he simply retracted his legs to render my efforts vain. And he was not the only one. I was surprised to find these children so affectionate. Christopher and Zachary, however, were of greatest interest to them. Children are fascinated with their own kind, especially with those who, a bit bigger than themselves, can give piggyback rides.

Our time up, Sasha led us back to the director's office, but not before informing us, through Viktor, that her birthday was approaching. Lauri and I suppressed smiles, but Christopher and Zachary, familiar with the tactic, laughed out loud. Sasha, thinking herself subtle, pretended not to notice.

ANOTHER MEETING WITH THE ORPHANAGE DIRECTOR AND THE process of adopting Sasha was formally initiated. You see, the purpose of this meeting, and of the witness from the AI's office, was to see if we wanted the child.

"Do you want her?" the orphanage director asked. Lauri and I were rather astonished by the question.

"Yes, we do."

We had traveled thousands of miles at great expense on no whim, but after a yearlong process. Still, it was required of them to ask the question and to have our answer on record. Should you answer yes, they proceed accordingly. Then you wait and visit your new child while the process grinds on through the government apparatus. The orphanage director determines what visitation rights you will be permitted. Some strictly limit those privileges. Others, more generous of heart, grant some latitude. Fortunately, the director of Orphanage #17 was just such a woman. Beginning the next day, Sasha would be allowed to visit us at our hotel.

"Do you understand this, Sasha?" the director asked. The little girl—our little girl—didn't say a word. She didn't have to. Her face, exultant, was her answer.

We left the orphanage with conflicting emotions. Meeting Sasha, providing her with hope, brought no small measure of joy to us all. But to see the conditions in which she and so many other children lived troubled us. Still, I left thanking God for those people, those Christians, who had labored anonymously and at their own expense to ease the hardships of these orphans. In so doing, they had ministered to our daughter.

FOUR

Show Me the Money

Be aware that corruption is widespread among Ukrainian police, and tourists are an especially profitable target.

—*Ukraine Travel Guide*[1]

THE NEXT DAY WAS CRISP AND CLEAR. SETTLING INTO OUR hotel—a small apartment, really—Lauri made the place feel as cozy as possible and prepared for Sasha's visit. Meanwhile, the boys and I explored the neighborhood, locating such essentials as Wi-Fi connectivity and McDonald's. Our apartment, just off of Deribasovskaya Street in the heart of the city, was perfectly located. The area looked something like the French Quarter in New Orleans, without the trashy element and Katrina flood damage. It was fashionable and clearly new.

Driving to the orphanage with Viktor would become part of a daily adventure for me. By any American standard, Viktor was an aggressive driver. By Ukrainian standards, he drove like an old lady, and that suited me fine. The Overseas Security Advisory Council warns travelers to Ukraine:

> Traffic laws are routinely disregarded by local drivers, i.e., excessive speeding, driving the wrong way on one-way streets, driving in oncoming lanes to maneuver around blocked traffic, and driving on sidewalks. Using sidewalks for parking is an accepted practice and pedestrians, especially those walking with small children, should exercise caution. Cars also routinely drive on sidewalks, especially in central Kyiv [Kiev], moving to and from sidewalk parking, much of it illegal. Ukrainian drivers will also stop in busy traffic lanes to frequent roadside kiosks or to pick up or drop off passengers . . . Defensive driving is a fundamental rule that should always be observed.[2]

This author knew his subject. To his observations I add my own: lines on the roads serve only a decorative purpose, since no one acknowledges them; cars may go three or even four wide on a two-lane; the shoulder of the road, if there is one, is for anybody who wants to use it; and bumper stickers tout more than one's political or social philosophy.

"What does that sticker with the *Y* on it mean?" I asked Viktor. "I have seen it on several cars."

"It means that the driver is learning," he said. "It means, 'Be careful of me. I may make a mistake.'" That seemed reasonable enough.

"What about that one?" I pointed out a bumper sticker with a high-heeled boot on it. I thought it was, like the lines on the road, decorative. But, no, it had an official purpose.

"That is for women drivers," he explained without a hint

of sarcasm. "If a man does something stupid on the road"—
I had noted several doing precisely that—"we will shout at
him." So far, this sounded like the American way. But there
was more. "If it is a woman, however, we will see that sticker
and understand. That sticker says, 'I am a woman. Be careful, because I may do something stupid.'" I tried to imagine
Nancy Pelosi or Barbara Boxer championing this kind of
sticker legislation in the United States, but it was too much.

Sasha was waiting for us excitedly when we arrived.
With hair pulled back in pigtails, she bounded through the
windswept courtyard to greet us. She told Viktor that she
was ready, but that the orphanage director wanted to see us
before we left. Walking to her office, I was again struck by
the desolate nature of the orphanage. I had ministered in
maximum security prisons with more warmth. No kidding.

The director spoke to Viktor. She seemed very serious
and did not wait for translation. Sasha listened and nodded.
I stood uncomprehending.

We left her office and made for the gate, solemnly.

"The director says that the adoption inspector must not
know that Sasha is being allowed to spend the afternoons with
your family at the apartment." Viktor sounded rather surrep-
titious. "She also sternly warned Sasha not to say a word about
it." Viktor shot a glance at Sasha, who seemed to intuit his
meaning even if the English words meant nothing to her.

On the way to the apartment, Sasha sat silently. Outside
of the surroundings she knew so well, she seemed less sure
of herself, if not altogether uneasy.

Photo by Larry Alex Taunton

Sasha's first day with us at our apartment in Odessa. Zachary (standing) and Christopher (kneeling) greeted her warmly.

"Sasha!" Lauri extended her arms and gathered Sasha up in a hug as she entered the apartment. Lauri had succeeded in giving the little three-room unit warmth. A hearty lunch sat on the table, music played softly in the background, and a number of little gifts awaited this newest member of our family. Sasha just wandered around the apartment, looking at things and asking questions. Viktor, ever present, translated. "She wants to know what that is," he said, amused. "I have explained to her that it is for making coffee."

At first, she just asked those kinds of basic questions—what is this and what is that? Finally, we all sat down for lunch, and I was astonished at her appetite. Slight of build, she ate her weight in whatever was offered. Christopher and Zachary exchanged smiles but said nothing. And so the day began.

In terms of our activities, there was nothing remarkable about Sasha's first visit with us. Even so, there was an otherworldly quality about it all. Walking around the city center, we found ourselves just following her and trying to experience things as she was experiencing them. She moved from shop window to shop window with a kind of Julie Andrews, *Sound of Music* twirl. Her eyes full of wonder, she was captivated by a Barbie doll in a grocery store. I bought it. That was my first Barbie purchase. Ever. Lauri mildly warned me not to spoil her. The point was well taken, but she was such an adorable little girl. Her big, green eyes, blond hair pulled back—it was hard to deny her anything.

By arrangement with the director, Sasha had to be returned to the orphanage each day by 7 p.m. Departing with Viktor, she reminded us that her birthday was approaching.

Again, the boys laughed. This time, she blushed and turned away with a bashful grin.

SASHA BEGAN VISITING OUR APARTMENT EVERY DAY. ALTHOUGH other children at the orphanage were in school, the orphanage director had decided that Sasha's attendance was no longer mandatory given the circumstances. So each morning, Viktor would pick Sasha up and deliver her to our apartment. Meanwhile, the procedural aspects of the adoption fell into a regular pattern of meetings, followed by the monotony of waiting for the next meeting.

Since we had formally declared our desire to adopt Sasha, we now had to return to the AI's office to initiate the process there. We arrived at the appointed time, but appointed times, I would discover, were meaningless. Since there were no waiting rooms, we usually opted to sit in the car. The interior of Viktor's Mitsubishi would become quite familiar to me. Bored, I began speculating whether or not the stereo was original equipment, and I organized his change holder.

Finally, the AI called Viktor and informed him that she would not provide us with the necessary documentation for another week.

"What is her reason for that?" I asked, knowing the answer to my own question. Viktor shrugged.

"She says that it is required." The silence that followed was awkward. Viktor knew what I was thinking but did not want to say it.

A historian by training, as a graduate student I had specialized in Russia and Eastern Europe. As a consequence, I had spent considerable time in that part of the world—Russia, the Czech Republic, Poland, Hungary, and Ukraine—and was not wholly unfamiliar with its business practices.

There really was no logical reason for this sudden delay in an already lengthy process, *unless*—

"Does she want a bribe, Viktor?" He looked startled and uncomfortable. This was a breach of etiquette. I was indifferent.

"Uh, a *gift* might be helpful." Viktor shifted nervously in his seat.

"Then do it," I ordered. "I trust you'll negotiate a good deal."

Viktor sprang from the car and went back inside. It was now close to 6 p.m., but from outside I could see that the AI's office was still illuminated. Perhaps she was waiting for us. She was not, I reasoned, a rookie in such matters.

Upon his return, Viktor appeared anxious. Such was his nature, but he clearly did not want to tell me what had transpired. Getting in the car, he turned to me.

"Did she accept it?" I asked impatiently.

"Yes, she did."

"Excellent! How much?"

"Uh . . . one hundred dollars."

Why wasn't Viktor pleased? That seemed like a bargain. One less week in Ukraine would save me several hundred dollars.

"Well done!" I congratulated him. Again, he seemed to squirm behind the steering wheel.

"Well, not exactly," he began. "She accepted the gift but still will not give us the document we need. She says that if she expedites our papers, it will attract the attention of her superiors, and they will think that she has taken a bribe."

I was dumbfounded.

"But she *did* take a bribe," I said flatly.

"Uh, well, yes." Viktor preferred the euphemism "gift." "But she doesn't want *them* to know it."

"Let me get this straight." I could feel a rising anger. "We have 'gifted' her to expedite this adoption—that is, to give us a paper that sits on her desk even now. But she isn't going to do it; is that right?" Viktor nodded, averting his eyes.

A Ukrainian adoption requires a series of sequential steps. The operative word here is *sequential*. You cannot move to step three until steps one and two are accomplished. The AI's refusal to provide us with a simple document would delay the adoption and Sasha's access to proper medical treatment by at least a week. And this was only the beginning.

FIVE

Haves and Have-nots

*There are only two families in the world, my
old grandmother used to say, the Haves and the
Have-nots.*

—MIGUEL DE CERVANTES

SINCE THE COLLAPSE OF THE SOVIET UNION IN 1991, EASTERN
Europe has been in a state of flux. I had noted the incre-
mental changes with every trip. When I first went to Russia
many years ago, capitalism was then only an idea that
the mafia took seriously. Now there is –or was, until the
recent recession—a booming economy, especially in those
countries like Ukraine that are former Soviet satellites.
Roads that were sparsely populated with Ladas and, for
the communist bosses, ZILs, are now bustling with Fords,
Lexuses, Volvos, Land Rovers, and just about any other
make or model you care to name. And shopping malls,
once strictly a Western phenomenon, are not only common but offer everything from Christian Dior to funnel
cakes. Indeed, while America is making the transition to

socialism, Eastern Europe is in the bare-knuckled stages of capitalism. Go figure.

Yes, that's bare-knuckled capitalism. Think robber barons, carpetbaggers, and haves and have-nots. According to the *Kyiv Post*: "The capital [of Ukraine's top fifty wealthiest individuals] is enough to finance the country's state budget for two years and comprises 85 percent of Ukraine's annual gross domestic product (GDP), whereas Russia's richest can only boast of covering 35 percent of their country's annual GDP."[1] In other words, the *haves* in Ukraine have almost everything.

Orphans are decidedly in the *have-not* category. Sitting in Viktor's all-too-familiar car at the orphanage, waiting to see the director, I decided to take a walk and inspect the compound. If I had been disheartened by what I had seen before, I was even more so by what I saw now. In a small outbuilding was the children's bathroom. There was no heat or air, no doors, and no stalls. There were only holes in the ground, the peripheries of each smeared with excrement and urine. And if that were not enough, the flies and the wretched smell made it intolerable. I snapped a few photos with my smartphone. That children used these bathrooms was appalling. Worse, the children were not even given toilet paper.

Being there on a daily basis, I also noticed that the children generally wore the same clothes day after day. When Sasha appeared at our apartment, wearing the same blue jeans, jacket, and sweater she had worn the two previous days, Lauri took matters into her own hands. First, she took Sasha shopping. After that, Lauri bathed her. Sasha had been accustomed to one shower per week. (That she got this was due to American short-term missionaries who constructed the orphanage shower.) When Sasha emerged, new clothes sat neatly folded on the bed, awaiting her selection. Finally, Lauri blow-dried and styled her hair. From that day forward, Sasha would luxuriate, almost purring, at this routine. It was as if the Cinderella story were being played out every day. For a little while, Sasha became a princess, and then, at midnight, the carriage became a pumpkin again.

The orphanage system bred children who were often characterized by a tough exterior. How could it do otherwise in a world where vulnerability was exploited? One could occasionally see it in the way the boys and girls carried themselves or in the way they talked. Sasha was not wholly immune to these effects, but when the opportunity presented itself, she became all *girl*. I cannot give that word content, so I will trust that you know what I mean. For example, one day the boys were walking with her through the mall when they realized she was no longer at their side. Doubling back, they found Sasha standing, wide-eyed, in front of a perfumery. On another occasion, Lauri sent me out to get a couple of items, and Sasha, tagging along, spotted barrettes with pink butterflies or some such thing on them. Needless to say, I bought them. And when she was given a choice of clothes, she always gravitated to the most feminine option.

Be it carriage by day or pumpkin by night, these visits

were nonetheless important for Sasha. We began to see very modest changes in her and in our relationships with her. She followed Christopher and Zachary wherever they went, played video games with them, and generally ran them ragged. This was a new and good experience for them. Girls were a species with which they were largely unfamiliar, and Sasha did not make her participation in their world optional.

She also became very comfortable with Lauri. Accustomed to female supervision, she readily yielded to Lauri's instructions and care. Sasha loved to help her in the kitchen, with grocery shopping, and with everything else.

More complex was her relationship with me. Ukraine is a matriarchal society, and the orphanages are matriarchal in the extreme. Women had dominated Sasha's world. Male children were not unknown to her, but men had only been in the background. Like extras in a play, they flitted across her life's stage every once in a while, but she never engaged them. And that was another thing—women seemed to run not only each individual orphanage, but the entire orphanage system. With the exception of the young man who supervised our meeting with Sasha, we would deal with women throughout the process, both in Kiev and in Odessa. Upon reflection, I became aware that women seemed to run the whole country. (Except for the mafia, of course, and everyone knows that they *really* run the country.)

Still, Sasha was drawn to me, if only out of curiosity. Whenever I left the apartment, she would ask why. If I retreated to one of the apartment's bedrooms to read or work, she would often sneak in, giggle, and run away. She liked helping me with Russian words, pronouncing them slowly and playfully mocking my efforts to repeat them. And when I returned from an errand, she would hide and call for me to look for her. In spite of all of this, however, she always maintained a certain distance. Occasionally, I caught her watching me. She would turn away with a shy smile. I suppose, in this respect, we were in the same boat. She was new to fathers, and I was new to daughters.

I often wished that we could see into her past so that we might better address her future. Lacking the ability to speak each other's language, however, severely limited communication. At this point, if we were to learn anything about her, it must be through observation. There was some modest advancement in her English (and in our Russian), but only enough to express the barest of things—what and where. But meaningful communication requires language, not hand gestures and pictures, if it is to bear the weight of ideas. So, to help Sasha's understanding of English, Lauri and I started taking her for walks around the city to expand her vocabulary. Passing an object for the first time, we would identify it in English. Passing it a second time, she was required to say it. *"Schto eta? Ska-zhee par Angleeski,"* we would say. ("What is this? Say it in English.") To begin with, she was uninterested, but recognizing in her a competitive nature, I decided to make it a game. For every object she named correctly, she got a point. For every incorrect answer, I got a point. She liked the game and sought to win. It was a strategy we would use again.

Our position with her, however, was awkward. She was entrusted to our care from 10 a.m. to 7 p.m. each day, and the orphanage was quick to tell us what she could and could not do. We had no real authority over her.

One afternoon we took her to McDonald's. That it was a treat for her was evident. She was very excited and insisted on ordering for herself. The poor woman at the register waited while Sasha considered all of the options for several minutes. Finally, she ordered what any one of us would have ordered for her—a Happy Meal. The next day the orphanage dorm supervisor chastised us.

"Ukrainian children do not eat bad food like American children," she said with something of a nationalistic edge. We were not, she declared, to feed Sasha McDonald's ever again.

That American children frequently eat poorly, I would hardly deny. What grated on us, however, was the implicit suggestion that the orphanage *really* had Sasha's best interests in mind, while we did not. Still, obedient to the supervisor's wishes, the next day we went to a deli where they served soups, salads, etc. Sasha, a typical child in this respect, didn't like it as much and didn't eat as much. Not a big deal, right? Once again, the dorm supervisor let us have it. This time, the charge was that we did not feed her enough.

The irony of all of this is that many of these orphanage bureaucrats don't really care about the children. That is, they don't care unless you want to adopt one of these children, and then nothing and no one is good enough. I remind you of the questions we were asked by the AI in our first meeting with her: "How many square meters is your home?" and "How much money do you make?" and "How many bedrooms do you have?" and "What is your occupation?" Questions like these and many others were asked with a distinct air of condescension.

You have got to be kidding me, I thought in retrospect. If Lauri and I lived in a double-wide, had only ten teeth between us, and ate SpaghettiOs for every meal, but truly loved the child, it would have been preferable to the conditions these children were living in now. It had all the charm of a chicken house. And as for love, I can only say that there was precious little of it for anyone in this society who could not fend for himself.

As one might imagine, Sasha seemed uncertain about where all of this was headed. Staying in the same apartment complex was another American family. From Pennsylvania, the Mortons were also in Ukraine to adopt. When they stopped by our apartment one day, we visited with them briefly. Philip and his wife, Michelle, had decided to adopt after they participated in a program sponsored by their church in Philadelphia whereby groups of Ukrainian orphans were brought to the United States for the summer. Their ten-year-old daughter, Jessica, had befriended one of them, and now, a year later, they had come to claim her.

Listening to their story, we momentarily forgot about

61

Sasha, who began talking animatedly with Viktor. Suddenly, she looked very distressed.

"What's wrong, Sasha?" Lauri asked. Sasha said nothing, but sat breathlessly.

"I do not know what is wrong with her," Viktor answered for her, palms up, as if inviting suggestions. "She wanted to know who the Mortons were, so I told her that they were here to adopt."

Suddenly, a wave of comprehension swept over Lauri's face.

"Viktor, please tell her that the Mortons are here to adopt a girl named Anya from Orphanage #5, not *her*."

Viktor did as he was instructed, and we saw Sasha exhale and slump in relief.

"I am sorry," Viktor said, chuckling. "She misunderstood me."

Apparently Sasha feared that we were pulling some sort of bait-and-switch routine. Sometimes distrust runs deep after a lifetime of betrayal.

No doubt contributing to this distrust were the rumors regarding internationally adopted children. When the Mortons' adoption inspector learned that Michelle Morton had a close relative with a serious kidney infection, she accused the Mortons of wanting to adopt so they could harvest the child's kidney. Appalled by this accusation, the Mortons protested the charge, only to discover that the AI was not interested in anything they might *say*. No, this AI, cut from the same cloth as our own, was much more interested in what they might *do*. A brief negotiation and "gift" later and they were back on track.

Of course, as we well knew, gifts didn't always jump-start the process. Our AI continued to sit on our case while Viktor and I sat outside in the car. Sometimes, a whole day would pass when, after repeated assurances to the contrary, we never saw her. And this wasn't even the hard part. After all, she had what we needed. What if she required us to track down Sasha's biological mother? That could be a long, if not impossible, task.

A cynical Russian proverb from the Soviet era describes the culture of socialism well: "We dig iron ore from the ground to make steel to make big machines that dig iron ore from the ground, to make steel to make big machines . . ." That there was a communist bureaucratic hangover in the old East Bloc was evident. This was reflected in the attitudes toward government and its role. Like any good American, I still labored under the quaint notion that government officials work for the taxpayer. In Ukraine, however, there was a nauseating obeisance, suggesting that while the KGB may be gone, it is not forgotten. From its earliest history, the people of Ukraine had been told what to do by one oppressive czarist or communist regime after another, and while attitudes were changing, it would take more than a couple of decades to undo the work of centuries.

SIX

The Devil Is a Bureaucrat

The bureaucratic mind-set is the only constant in the universe.

—DR. MCCOY, *STAR TREK IV*

THAT GREAT PHILOSOPHER TOM PETTY KNEW WHAT HE WAS talking about when he wrote, "The waiting is the hardest part." And he probably penned that line at Club Med while waiting for one of those drinks with a little umbrella in it. Ukraine ain't Club Med. The Ukrainian experience breeds a whole different kind of philosophical reflection. Hence, optimistic Ukrainian proverbs such as, "Those sitting above can easily spit on those below" and "Love well, whip well." Historically, there has been a lot of spitting and whipping in that country.

As a result of our experience there, I had made a great theological breakthrough. It is said that Martin Luther made his while using the toilet. I made mine while photographing one at the orphanage. My discovery? *The devil is a bureaucrat.* I am confident that hell will be full of such people.

Dante thought so too. According to his hierarchy, corrupt politicians are in the eighth circle of hell. For the uninitiated, that's near the bottom, as there were only nine circles. Above them, in less torturous circumstances, he put cowards, heretics, usurers, blasphemers, and even murderers. My guess is, Dante stood in one government line too many before going postal in the literary sense. "Abandon all hope ye who enter here," reads the sign over the entrance to Dante's Inferno. It is said that similar signs greet Cubs fans at Wrigley Field and anyone entering a Ukrainian government building.

JESSICA MORTON BECAME SOMETHING OF A FIXTURE WITH Sasha and our boys. The foursome filled their days with board games, errands for their mothers, and exploring Deribasovskaya Street. One day Jessica excitedly informed the boys that she and her family would be going home soon. Philip, Jessica's father, confirmed this bit of good news, telling me that their court date to finalize the adoption was scheduled just a few days hence. Delighted that he could stop the monetary hemorrhage and return to work in Philadelphia, he was visibly cheered.

Then, inexplicably, the court date was canceled. One government official, doing his best to keep up the spit-and-whip tradition, bluntly informed Philip that he would not approve the adoption unless Philip paid him $600. Having no alternative, Philip forked over the money, and the man signed. We puzzled over the odd figure—$600. That was 4,830 hryvnia according to the current exchange rate. Why not make it a round number, like $500 or $1,000? We decided that he had something specific in mind, like a new flat or, better yet, a visa out of the country. No doubt, someone above had spit on him, so he decided to spit on Philip.

The bureaucracy we encountered in Odessa was worthy of at least the sixth circle of Dante's hell (heretics). Initially, one is inclined to think—especially if one is an American—that the corruption is confined to a few officials. *If only I can get past them*, you reason to yourself. Such was my thinking with the AI. Eventually, however, it dawns on you that the corruption is systemic.

Our hotel, for example, was advertised as "American Owned." We chose the place for its location. But being owned by an American was definitely a point of emphasis in their advertisements. So what does that get you? Nothing. At check-in the receptionist said to me in broken English, "You pay full amount now."

"What?" I protested. "Don't we pay when we check out? We don't even know how long we will be staying."

She was emphatic. "No, you pay now. It is the Ukrainian way."

"But doesn't that defeat the point of being 'American owned'?"

She feigned misunderstanding. I paid half. Her understanding of English improved dramatically as she explained the nuances of Ukrainian business practices. This time, I feigned misunderstanding.

"You pay at check-in here," the owner, overhearing us from an adjoining room, explained. "But when you check out, if you haven't stayed for the full time, we will refund any remaining money."

I remained dubious and, it turned out, for good reason. Upon checkout, she refused to refund what was clearly owed to me.

"We don't give refunds," she said with a completely straight face. I explained flatly that the money was owed and reminded her that we had discussed this at check-in. Again, her boss overheard us and intervened.

"We will give you a credit; how about that?" He seemed proud of his magnanimity.

"I don't want a credit," I insisted. "I want my money."

"Don't you plan to come back to Odessa?" He gestured expansively, as though this were *Fantasy Island* and he Mr. Roarke.

"Not if I can help it."

He reached into his pants and produced a wad of cash. After some tense discussion, he offered to refund *half* of my money and to give me a credit that I would never use for the other half. Having no meaningful recourse, I accepted.

Then again, maybe he was fulfilling fantasies after all—the hotel, we discovered, was operating an escort service. Young ladies coming and going on the arms of fat, middle-aged businessmen was a frequent sight. And all of this—the corruption, the exploitation of young women, the absence of meaningful civil laws to protect the rights of the powerless—is very much in keeping with what can be seen in the former East Bloc, Russia and Ukraine in particular.

According to *Forbes* magazine, Ukraine is one of the worst places in the world to do business because of rampant corruption.[1] This report was largely based on the findings of Transparency International, a nonprofit dedicated to exposing global corruption. Each year Transparency International ranks countries from least to most corrupt on their "Corruption Index." Out of 180 entries, Ukraine ranks 134th. In other words, 133 countries were deemed less corrupt than Ukraine. Ukraine ranks well behind such models of integrity as Nicaragua, Vietnam, and Rwanda. Mexico is listed a full 36 spots *ahead* of Ukraine. Of course, Ukraine was well schooled. Russia, tutor and master to Ukraine for centuries, is ranked even worse, at 154th. And they probably had to bribe someone to get *that* spot.[2]

In spite of these facts, Western businessmen are not uncommon. Many are legit. Whether they are representatives of large, well-known companies, small firms, or individuals, all are banking on Ukraine's potential and have sought to develop it since the collapse of the Soviet Union. Their efforts have not all been in vain. But there is an altogether different sort of Western businessman that is also common in Ukraine. He is a type that is attracted to Ukraine precisely because of the absence of certain legal restrictions, and not because he has a Jeffersonian view of government. It is, rather, because his designs are immoral, and as long as he has the money to buy off the right people, he will be given a free hand to do as he pleases.

"So, why did you decide to move to Ukraine?" I asked an American entrepreneur who was just this sort. Seedy looking and in his late fifties, he was accompanied by his Ukrainian mistress, who stood scantily clad in a miniskirt and a blouse with a plunging neckline.

"The tax laws," he said, affecting an air of sophistication. The girl appeared to be in her teens. *No*, I thought, *you are avoiding statutory rape laws.*

"Cumulatively, I figure I pay less in bribes here than I do in taxes in New Yawwk." His accent was pronounced. "It's kind of like the Old West here."

"Sounds more like the Old East, to me," I observed. *Because they probably would have hanged you in the Old West*, I added, to myself. He smiled uncomprehendingly. (By "Old East," I meant business as usual in this part of the world.)

Walking through a computer store one day with Viktor, I whistled absentmindedly as we browsed. Viktor turned to me and said quietly, but with great seriousness, "Don't whistle inside buildings. In Ukraine, it is considered bad luck." That explained a lot. A brief reflection on Ukraine's history and I concluded that the whole country had been whistling inside for centuries. Consider the following . . .

In sharp contrast to the linear, progressive histories of Western Europe and America, Ukraine's story has been one of cycles. Bad cycles. Lacking any natural borders behind which its people might have taken refuge, Ukraine has been a doormat to invading armies from both East and West since time immemorial. First came the Vikings, or Varangians, as they are referred to in *The Primary Chronicle*, Ukraine's earliest native historical source. They moved up and down Ukraine's rivers as if they owned the place. And, well, eventually they did.

Next were the Mongols. They galloped onto the Ukrainian steppe in 1241 and, deciding they liked it, stayed for more than two centuries. Unfortunately, they were not much for painting *matryoshka* dolls or Ukrainian folk dancing. Instead, they passed the time pillaging and burning Ukrainian villages. A nasty, ruthless, and uncivilized people, the Mongols brought nothing worthy of imitation, except their methods of warfare. The Ukrainians mimicked them in everything but warfare. As a consequence, they became a nasty, ruthless, and uncivilized people who were sissy slapped by everyone with whom they came into contact—Turks, Poles, Turks again, Lithuanians, Swedes, Turks again, Russians, Germans, Russians again, Germans again, Russians again, etc.

Somewhere along the way, the proverb "Those sitting above can easily spit on those below" made its appearance in Ukraine. Drenched in the saliva of foreigners and unscrupulous, homegrown thugs, someone finally decided that it was time for Ukrainians to stop indoor whistling. Fortunes changed, and in 1991, Ukraine managed independence for the first time in its long and tragic history.

And what a long and tragic history it has been. Conquest, occupation, enslavement, state-engineered famines, collectivization, purges, fascism, communism, nuclear disasters—Ukraine has experienced them all. If ever a country deserved a break, it is this one. And yet, there is a growing number of Ukrainians who are nostalgic for the past. Some Ukrainians want to reunite with Russia—16 percent of them, according to a recent poll, with many more sympathetic to the idea. Granted, that number is a long way from a majority, but still, sixteen out of every hundred? Can you imagine a similar number of, say, Republicans longing for the Carter era? On second thought, scratch that question.

Throughout all of these many changes, there has been one constant—a *corrupt bureaucracy*. But modern Ukraine has an opportunity to reform that none of its forebears ever had. The growing desire to go back to Egypt, however, is worrying. "A dog," reads Proverbs 26:11, "returns to its vomit."

SEVEN

A Brief (and Mostly True) History of Religion in Ukraine

Drinking is the joy of the Russes!

—FROM *THE PRIMARY CHRONICLE*

HISTORIANS HAVE LONG REGARDED 988 AS ONE OF THE MOST fateful dates in the history of Eastern Europe. It was in that year that Vladimir, prince of Kievan Rus (think modern Russia and Ukraine), converted to Greek Orthodoxy. The consequences were far-reaching and devastating in effect. Here's how it happened . . .

Paganism was passé among the civilized peoples of Europe, and Kievan Rus needed a change. According to *The Primary Chronicle*, Prince Vladimir sent out emissaries to investigate the major religious options then available. They considered Judaism and Islam in addition to Greek and Roman Christianity. When his emissaries returned, Vladimir listened attentively to their accounts, weighing the pros and cons of each religion. Islam, it seems, was in the running until Vladimir was told that Muslims are not permitted to drink alcohol. His response was emphatic: "Drinking is the joy of the Russes!" Here we have the only instance in the recorded history of Ukraine and Russia where a ruler of those countries made a decision that truly reflected the will of the people. Attaboy, Vlad. Besides, with Ukraine holding an important place in the "Vodka Belt," they had their reputation to consider.

"To our health!" Vladimir declared, throwing back some of this firewater, melting his liver and other vital organs. (Interestingly, the old Ukrainian name for vodka is *horilka*, or *goryashchee*, from the Slavonic root meaning "to burn." This is probably because observers discovered a direct correlation between vodka consumption and the destruction of public and private property.)

Judaism was presented next for his consideration, but the bit about circumcision made him shift uncomfortably on his throne. "Nyet!" he declared, cutting off the spokes-man midsentence. Crossing his legs, Vladimir asked the emissaries who went to Germany what the Catholics had to offer, but they gave what he regarded as an equally unim-pressive report. Yes, drinking was permitted, beer being the drink of choice. Still, they said, "We beheld no glory there." It seems that for these boys to see glory, they needed the kind of buzz only vodka can provide.

Zero for three, things didn't look too promising when the fellows who went to Constantinople to appraise Greek Orthodoxy spoke up. Having visited Hagia Sophia before the Ottomans trashed it, they were overawed by what they saw there. "We knew not whether we were in heaven or on earth . . . we know only that God dwells there among men." *The Primary Chronicle* further states that the Byzantine emperors Basil II and Constantine VIII lavished them with great gifts. Unfortunately, it does not record what these gifts were, but it has long been speculated that gold, spices, and an autographed copy of *"Yanni's Greatest Hits"* were among them. Although deeply impressed, Vladimir still had reservations. Stroking his beard thoughtfully, his eyes narrowing, he gazed skeptically as he asked the Greek position on vodka and circumcision. The first was permissible, they said, and the second not required. Vladimir's eyebrows shot up in surprise. This sounded an awful lot like paganism . . . Thus, Vladimir knew this was the religion for him!

Converting to Greek Orthodoxy, Vladimir became a lover of all things Greek. So much so that he immediately declared war on Constantinople in an effort to possess it. The Greeks explained to him that this really wasn't a very Christian thing to do. It seems that he had misunderstood what Christians meant by "sword drill." He needed baptism, they said. Vladimir agreed. He then enthusiastically required all of his subjects, under penalty of death, to be baptized too. Vlad made a lot of converts this way. Publicly, the Greeks declared him a saint. Privately, they considered him a slow learner.

So why was 988 such a disaster? The adoption of Greek Orthodoxy forever separated Ukraine and Russia from the

Western world culturally and linguistically. Hence, they never experienced the Renaissance, the Reformation, the Enlightenment, the Scientific Revolution, the Industrial Revolution, or the French man-purse craze. By the twentieth century, these countries lagged behind the West by a good two centuries. The earliest rumblings of the Industrial Revolution could be heard in England in the 1740s. They would not be heard in Ukraine in earnest until the first of the Five-Year Plans in 1928.

What were the theological implications? Greek Orthodoxy, as practiced by the Russians, has had a history of xenophobia, a strong strain of anti-Semitism, and otherworldliness in the extreme. It is a religion without grace, of ritual obedience, with little connection to the Bible, and worship of an impersonal god who is unknown and unknowable. In other words, it is typically not very Christian.

The keystone that sits atop the grand archway of authentic Christianity is grace. By it and it alone does one gain access to Jesus Christ and, by him, to God the Father and eternal life. Remove it and the whole edifice collapses, no matter what features of Christianity may remain. Without grace the sacraments are not sacramental and the preaching of God's Word serves no purpose beyond reminding the patient that he has a disease for which there is no cure. Without grace, Christianity is reduced to mere religion and is as hollow as the many Orthodox cathedrals and churches that, today, are little more than tourist attractions.

EIGHT

"Imagine There's No Heaven"

Atheists in Charge of the Twentieth Century

*Okay, suppose there is no hope. Suppose there is
no justice. Suppose there's nothing but misery and
darkness and bleakness. Suppose there's nothing
that we would wish for, nothing that we would
hope for. Too bad!*

—RICHARD DAWKINS

RUSSIAN SOCIALISTS DID MORE THAN IMAGINE THE GODLESS
world John Lennon sang about and Richard Dawkins
spoke of—*they built it.* For more than seventy-five years,
the world's atheistic elites had their way with foreign and
domestic policy, the military and secret police, the economy,
and the lives of millions of people. The result? Seven decades
of unremitting turmoil, bloodshed, famine, theft, backward-
ness, incompetence, and promises of a coming utopia.

A socialist state is no utopia. Strictly speaking, socialism is a phase on the way to a utopia called *communism*,

and that, as every sensible person knows, is about as utopian as, well, a day in any communist country you care to name. "Communists," John F. Kennedy observed, "have never come to power in any country that was not disrupted by war, internal repression, or both."[1] More than that, war and internal repression are the chief means of *maintaining* power. Well, that and a Kalashnikov aimed squarely at the unfortunate citizens of the country in question. Vladimir Lenin, a godless maniac, said, "Under socialism, all will govern in turn, and will soon become accustomed to no one governing."[2] *All* must have a much more exclusive meaning in Russian than in English because Lenin limited governance to himself. When Lenin died, Joseph Stalin, following his predecessor's example, also limited power to himself. Khrushchev, defining *all* more liberally, decided to spread the joy and included a few of his drinking comrades, and so it continued until the collapse of the Soviet Union in 1991. Lenin was, however, right about one thing—it did seem as if no one were in charge. Indeed, to observe government in a socialist country is to witness the Peter Principle at work on a national scale.[3]

But the failure of socialism is not only a wholly unjustified confidence in human government. Socialism begins with a premise that is antithetical to Christianity: *there is no God.* Fyodor Dostoevsky observed this connection between atheism and socialism long ago: "Socialism is not merely the labour question, it is before all things the atheistic question, the question of the form taken by atheism today, the question of the tower of Babel built without God, not to mount to Heaven from earth, but to set up Heaven on earth."[4]

In other words, socialism is much more than an economic or political question. It is a *spiritual* question if only because it denies the very existence of the spiritual.[5]

A former socialist revolutionary, Dostoevsky knew his subject well. Upon his conversion to Christianity, he did more than renounce his atheism; he renounced socialism, because it was, in his view, atheism masquerading as political philosophy. In his great novels *Demons* (also known as *The Possessed*) and *The Brothers Karamazov*, Dostoevsky predicted that if Russia's communists (think, socialists) ever gained control of the levers of power, it would lead to the expulsion of Christianity from public life, and with it, the annihilation of morality, the rise of totalitarianism, and the proliferation of state-sponsored genocide. He would prove prophetic.

I am, of course, well aware of the fact that there are many who confuse socialism with Christianity. Such people usually have only a cursory understanding of what one or the other really is. Typically, this is predicated on the erroneous notion that Christianity's chief purpose is in meeting physical needs. This is not so. Christianity's main object is the regeneration and development of the soul. That Christianity and socialism are often confused, however, has not escaped the attention of socialists who have frequently sought to capitalize on the misunderstanding. As for "Christian Socialism," it is only a name. One may be a Christian or he may be a socialist; but he can no more be a Christian and a socialist than he can be both a Yankees and a Red Sox fan. At least, he cannot be simultaneously faithful to each party.

Indeed, far from being compatible with Christianity, socialist regimes have historically sought the expulsion of Christianity from public life. Christianity, by its very nature, is subversive insofar as it teaches that there is a God whose laws supersede those of man—*any* man. "No totalitarian authority nor authoritarian state," wrote the late Francis Schaeffer, "can tolerate those who have an absolute by which to judge that state and its actions."[6] This goes far to explain the antipathy of communist and fascist regimes to Christianity. They well understand that Christians do not recognize the power of the state as absolute. Moreover, where temporal law and eternal law are in conflict, the Christian may, in good conscience, violate the former while clinging to the latter. It is much to the better that many have done so. History is full of examples of courageous Christian men and women who, at the risk of their own lives, sought the destruction of evil laws and regimes. By contrast, socialism exalts the state *in the place of* God. This stands in opposition to a traditional American view of government, where, as Alexis de Tocqueville observed more than a century ago, "as soon as a man has acquired some education and pecuniary resources . . . all that he asks of the state is not to be disturbed in his toil."[7] And while American government has at no time been Christian, it has historically respected the role Christianity has played in public life. Socialism, however, by making the state both the means and the end, violates the very first commandment: *You shall have no other gods before me.** It then proceeds to violate the other nine with wild abandon.

One might reasonably wonder how a country where the Orthodox Church held such a prominent position in the culture could become the bastion of all things godless. In his book *A People's Tragedy*, Cambridge historian Orlando Figes makes a profound observation regarding the communist takeover in Russia. He states that the triumph of Marxism (think, socialism) in 1917 Russia can in no small measure be attributed to the fact that there were *no viable competing ideologies*. Marxism had, in effect, been set loose in an ideological vacuum. The cultural bloodletters of the time had successfully drained Russia of what little defensive mechanisms it had in the first place. Thus, when Bolshevism (think, socialism) was injected into the body politic, the disease spread with little resistance. This reflects poorly on the Orthodox Church at the time. Having become wedded to the autocratic czarist regime, the Church's role was largely one of ceremony and preserving the status quo. Count Sergei Witte, once prime minister and modernizer of Russia, wrote on the eve of the Revolution:

---

* Interestingly, I once asked Richard Dawkins what he found objectionable about the Ten Commandments. He went straight to Exodus 20:3 and the opening line of the Decalogue.

> If one takes a long-view of the future, then, in my opin-
> ion, the greatest danger facing Russia comes from the sad
> state of the Orthodox Church and the decline in genuine
> religious spirit . . . Without a truly living church to give
> [spiritual ideals] expression, religion becomes philosophy
> and is unable to influence life. Without religion, the masses
> turn into beasts, worse than four-legged beasts because
> humans possess intelligence. Our church has turned into a
> dead, bureaucratic institution, and its services are conducted
> not to celebrate the God in heaven, but the earthly gods.
> Orthodoxy has become a kind of paganism. Herein lies our
> greatest danger. We have gradually become less Christian.[8]

Meanwhile, the activities of other Christian denomina-
tions were severely restricted by the state to the point that
they were a cultural nonfactor, and that, as history would
prove, was tragic.

If Russians and Ukrainians thought life under the czars
was tough—and it unquestionably was—the communists
would introduce them to horrors so vast in scale that it
beggars the imagination. Figures vary wildly, but by con-
servative estimates no fewer than 60 million people would
lose their lives between 1917 and 1991 under Soviet (think,
socialist) rule. Where did the utopian dream go wrong?

However attractive it may be to say so, it is inaccurate
to suggest that all of those who worked and, in some cases,
gave their lives to bring about socialist regimes in Russia
and a dozen other countries were all murderous brigands.

At least, most did not start that way, whatever their end. On the contrary, many sincerely believed that the system was the answer to mankind's problems of peace, bread, and land. Historian Sheila Fitzpatrick characterizes the socialist revolutionary spirit very well:

> All revolutions have liberté, égalité, fraternité, and other noble slogans inscribed on their banners. All revolutionaries are enthusiasts, zealots; all are utopians, with dreams of creating a new world in which the injustice, corruption, and apathy of the old world are banished forever. They are intolerant of disagreement; incapable of compromise; mesmerized by big, distant goals; violent, suspicious, destructive. . . . They have the intoxicating illusion of personifying the will of the people, which means they assume the people is monolithic. They are Manicheans, dividing the world into two camps: light and darkness, the revolution and its enemies. They despise all traditions, received wisdom, icons, and superstition. They believe society can be tabula rasa on which the revolution will write.
>
> It is the nature of revolutions to end in disillusionment and disappointment. . . . All revolutions destroy things whose loss is soon regretted.[9]

It is the nature of socialist revolutions to end in "disillusionment and disappointment" because, as we have already noted, they begin with the wrong premise—*there is no God*. Hence, socialism's whole trajectory hits wide of the intended mark. And how could it do otherwise? In the biblical world-view, the state is a temporal institution meant to serve man, an eternal being. In the socialist model, this is reversed: man, a temporal being, serves the eternal state.

In spite of any similarities that the New Atheists may share with the Bolsheviks—and there are quite a few*—it is not my point to suggest that the New Atheists are would-be socialist revolutionaries. Outside of Christopher Hitchens, whose opinions appear regularly in *Vanity Fair*, *Slate*, and the *Atlantic*, their political views are largely unknown to me. It is, rather, to demonstrate their extraordinary naïveté on matters of history. To read Richard Dawkins on history is—I shall endeavor to be kind—to venture into the idiotic. It is as if the secular atrocities of the twentieth century never happened. Indeed, it is as if the eighteenth century never happened.

Reading *The God Delusion* and listening to Dawkins's first debate with John Lennox in Birmingham, Alabama, could give you the distinct impression that Dawkins *really thinks* that a society based on atheism is an original idea. Perhaps he doesn't know any better. Someone should tell him.

In his farewell address in September 1796, George Washington offered a warning to his fellow citizens: "And let us with caution indulge the supposition that morality can be maintained without religion. Whatever may be conceded to the influence of refined education on minds of peculiar structure, reason and experience both forbid us

---

* In addition to atheism, perhaps their most striking similarity is that both claim to be "scientific."

to expect that national morality can prevail in exclusion of religious principle."*

Washington was not simply playing to the masses by tossing them this morsel of religious rhetoric. He was, I suspect, referring to a dangerous European experiment, the French Revolution, which sought the destruction of the Church and institutionalized atheism. The experiment was a failure. What followed included regicide, civil war, and the Reign of Terror. Deciding that belief in something beyond oneself might, after all, be a good idea, those clever social engineers of the Committee of Public Safety (a misnomer if ever there was one) responded with a half measure, creating the ridiculous "Cult of the Supreme Being" in 1794. It, too, was a failure. Washington was well aware of these events and recognized the pitiless nature of a godless society.

The French Revolution was, however, only history's first attempt at an entirely secular state. Perhaps subsequent generations would recognize the failure and move on. They did nothing of the sort. Instead, the French Revolution would become to socialists what Woodstock is to '60s burnouts. To the rest of us, both may be described in one word: *overrated*.

At the Oxford University Museum of Natural History, I chaired a second debate between Dawkins and Lennox. This time, Richard was in front of a home crowd and was, consequently, much less reticent to express his real

---

* At the 2009 National Prayer Breakfast in Washington, D.C., keynote speaker and former British prime minister Tony Blair gave an address that echoed these sentiments.

opinions. When Lennox pushed him on the meaningless-ness of his worldview, Dawkins replied, "Okay, suppose there is no hope. Suppose there is no justice. Suppose there's nothing but misery and darkness and bleakness. Suppose there's nothing that we would wish for, nothing that we would hope for. Too bad!'"

Following the debate, an audience member referred to this very statement and asked me, "Is Dawkins that men-dacious, or is he just not that bright after all?" The query is justified. Such a remark would seem to indicate that Dawkins has not given a moment's thought to where that sort of worldview leads—no, *has led*—and that is none other than the gallows, the Gulag, or the gas chamber. Of course, in the ivory tower of North Oxford, one can, I sup-pose, afford to be intellectually irresponsible. And that's precisely what it is—irresponsible. With just that sort of reasoning, Machiavelli armed tyrants and genocidal nut jobs from Lorenzo de' Medici to Joseph Stalin.

After the Oxford debate, my son Christopher, who was in attendance at the museum, told me that when Dawkins made this comment, he saw a group of Oxford students sniggering. "I wanted to go and stand in their midst and say, 'Why are you laughing?'" he explained. "'Didn't you hear what he said? He just told you that your life has no mean-ing.'" Having spent much of my professional life engaging students, I can say without hesitation that they, more than

---

* This debate is available on the Fixed Point Foundation website: www.fixed-point.org.

any other demographic, are quick to put legs to half-baked ideas. As I said, it is irresponsible. One cannot go over a waterfall only halfway.

Ironically, atheists like Dawkins and Hitchens regularly denounce the evils of communist regimes like that of North Korea. They do so for two reasons. First, they have been heavily influenced by a Judeo-Christian worldview that still informs many of their moral sentiments. Second, they have wrongly identified the ideological source of the problem in these countries. Atheism is not, as they would suggest, merely incidental to these regimes. It is integral to the system, because all good communists are, by definition, atheists. And that is what permits these governments to treat their citizens as commodities. Instead of a moral and teleological being made in the image of God, as in the Christian view, man is deemed to be nothing more than a soulless animal. As a consequence, there is no consideration for man's innate religious impulse or for his nonmaterial needs—and scarce consideration for his material ones.

Nowhere was this warped thinking more evident than in the system of orphanages devised during the Soviet era—and still in use today.

NINE

The Orphanage Archipelago

"Murder kills only the individual—and, after all, what is an individual?" With a sweeping gesture he indicated the rows of microscopes, the test-tubes, the incubators. "We can make a new one with the greatest ease—as many as we like."

—FROM ALDOUS HUXLEY'S *BRAVE NEW WORLD*[1]

Finding themselves in such a world at the dawn of their existence, so young, so defenseless, what must go on in these souls fresh from God?

—FROM VICTOR HUGO'S *LES MISÉRABLES*

THERE IS A SIMPLE MEANS FOR DETERMINING THE GOODNESS of any society, and it is not found in economic or political terms. It is in this: how do they treat their poor, their widowed, and their orphaned? In this sense, the orphanages were simply a microcosm of society, a random sample, so to speak, by which we might measure the virtue of the whole.

Our experiences in Ukraine had given us a glimpse into the country's societal soul, but there was much we still did not know—or was it that we didn't want to know?

Viktor went home to Lviv for a well-deserved rest and visit with his family. Coming off the bench in his absence was his colleague Arkady Romanenko. Arkady presented an interesting figure. His dress and style were that of a hip Eastern European, which may be briefly described as a black ensemble with bling accents. Although younger than Viktor, he had been an adoption facilitator longer, and it showed. Though his smile was charming, he nonetheless had an air of detachment about him, seeming a bit indifferent to the children he encountered. And where Viktor treated us as guests in his native country, Arkady regarded us as foreigners. The difference, though subtle, is not insignificant.

Still, we enjoyed him. Each day when he brought Sasha, he would stay for a cup of coffee or tea. Sitting in our little apartment's living room one afternoon, he spoke of America and his interaction with Christians from there. "I like them," he said. That was a good thing, since American evangelicals comprised almost all of his business.

"I even listen to some of their preachers. But I especially like their music." A smooth operator, Arkady was all things to all people. But that did not prevent him from speaking bluntly. As we quizzed him on his professional experiences, he demolished any hopes we might have still had that things weren't really as bad in Orphanage #17 as they appeared to be.

"What is your opinion of #17, Arkady?" Lauri asked.

Momentarily, Arkady looked at the floor and then said, "You don't want to know." Prevailed upon, though, he did not hold back.

"That orphanage is one of the worst that I have ever seen," he began. "There are some that are worse, especially in the countryside. But . . ." A thought interrupted him, one that would, perhaps, summarize the whole of his argument. "Have you seen the toilets?" His eyebrows were raised, inviting a response. I nodded. "Terrible," he said. "Not normal conditions."

But that was not all. "They have virtually no rules at #17." The place, he said, operated according to the rules established by the children themselves. "Jungle law," he called it. "The children there speak disrespectfully, using bad language with me, with each other, with their caregivers, with anyone," he said. "Worse, their caregivers talk just like them! The English equivalents to 'f— this' and 'f— that' always coming out of their mouths." Of course, this was unknown to us because we didn't speak Russian.

"When I can"—Arkady leaned forward in his chair and rested his elbows on his knees—"I like to observe the activities at the various orphanages. Sometimes they don't even notice that I'm there." Till then, Lauri had been cleaning the kitchen, but she sat down now to listen more carefully.

"The orphanage directors are responsible for two things," he continued. "Maintaining order and making provision for the physical needs of the children. Neither is done very well at #17." His back stiffened momentarily. "Watching the kids eat, there have been times when I have had to cover my nose from the stench because the food is rotten." He waved his hand in front of his face and grimaced. "I don't know where they get that food." I briefly recalled the reprimand we received for taking Sasha to McDonald's. The hypocrisy was even worse than I had thought.

"If it is food that they really want, I've seen children spit on it as soon as they get it so that no one else will take it."

Arkady went on to explain how the children were fed on a strict routine, the same things week after week, month after month, year after year. "You could ask Sasha what she is having for lunch next Friday and she will be able to tell you." Testing this theory, I told him to ask her. She was sitting nearby, playing Uno with the boys, not understanding a word of what we were saying. Putting the question to her, she paused thoughtfully and then said (in Russian), "A little meat and cabbage," before slapping down a Draw four. Arkady smiled.

"See? It is like this at every orphanage in Ukraine. They are run according to old Soviet principles." *No*, I thought, *they are run* without *principles*.

Arkady's description did much to explain Sasha's fixation with food and the fact that she ate her weight whenever she was with us. Sasha was a mite, weighing in at sixty pounds soaking wet. A stiff west Texas wind might have blown her away like tumbleweed. At dinner the night before, she had eaten a bowl of hearty chicken and vegetable soup, a salami sandwich, pasta salad, and topped it off with a big bowl of chocolate ice cream. To offer some perspective, I ate a bowl of soup and a modest helping of the pasta salad.

Before dinner, she worked excitedly in the kitchen, helping Lauri prepare the food. Never has a meal been lavished with more love and attention. She looked a little like one of those children in Willy Wonka's chocolate factory. But only a little. Where those kids were drooling over Everlasting Gobstoppers and other exotic candies, Sasha looked with similar excitement at much more pedestrian foods—onions, chicken, milk, corn, tomatoes, butter, and so forth. Those things never excited me too much as a child, as they were as common to our table as the salt and pepper on the lazy Susan.

But the deficiencies went well beyond the quality and quantity of the food at #17. During the week that Arkady substituted for Viktor, twice he had arrived at the orphanage to find Sasha in tears. "This last time I asked what happened," he explained. "One of the caregivers was sitting right there on a bench and said nothing. When one of the kids started to tell me, another said, 'Shut up! We don't talk about those things.' The caregiver just ignored it all." Finally, someone told Arkady that a teenage boy had attacked Sasha.

"No one cares at #17," he concluded. Of course, few cared at any of the orphanages. The system virtually guaranteed it.

How did things get like this? It may surprise you to know that it was not by accident. On the contrary, it took a lot of effort and coordination to screw things up this badly.

The answer is found in Arkady's off-handed remark: "They are run according to old Soviet principles." While the USSR has been consigned to the trash heap of history, it would be naive to assume that its influence ended in 1991. Economic policies, educational philosophies, political institutions, and so on did not change overnight. Indeed, many did not change at all. Nowhere was Soviet influence greater than in the orphanages. They provided a perfect laboratory for the educational theories of communist diehards like Anatoly Lunacharsky and Anton Makarenko.

As communists go, Lunacharsky is generally regarded as a warm-and-fuzzy type. This is probably because we have no record of Anatoly shooting anyone. That and the fact that Stalin did not like him, and nowadays this puts you in good standing with the millions of people who believe communism is a good idea that Stalin perverted. But make no mistake about it: Lunacharsky spiritually assassinated generations of Eastern European children with his soul-destroying communist educational theories.

When the Bolsheviks seized power in Russia in 1917, Lunacharsky was made Soviet commissar for education and the arts, a post he would maintain until 1929. And while he and Lenin (and later, Stalin) did not agree on the finer points of their doctrines, they did agree on a few basics: there was no God, no soul, no afterlife, and the supreme responsibility of the state was to make good communists. In Lunacharsky's view, the way to make good communists was for the state to usurp the role of parents:

"If we can overcome our poverty, I would say that the children's home is the best way of raising children—a genuine socialist upbringing, removing children from the family setting and its petty-bourgeois structure."[2] Overcoming national poverty is something socialists have never accomplished. Indeed, their economic policies achieve something akin to the opposite of the Midas touch, creating want where there had previously been none. Even so, the commissar, intoxicated by his grand vision, hoped to build a whole network of homes for all Soviet children, not just the orphaned or abandoned ones. He genuinely believed that the state could do a better job of raising children than mothers and fathers.

Soon it became clear, however, that the gap between the state's enthusiasm for this plan and its actual ability to carry it out was oceanic. The children who were without homes— a result of World War I, the Bolshevik coup d'état, a civil war, and a state-induced famine—numbered in the millions. Any plans that called for the seizure of children who already had a home were obviously unworkable. Not that practical considerations have often restrained bad governments from implementing bad policies, but this time the bureaucrats couldn't avoid noticing the scale of their problem. Homeless children, called *besprizornye* (a derogatory term meaning, literally, "ones without oversight"), roamed the streets, begged in train stations, and slept in trash bins. "Who has not seen them?" complained one old Bolshevik.[3]

State-run homes for these children were established

with the view that the government would rehabilitate and eventually graduate their charges as communists ready to serve the collective. Proper socialist indoctrination was all these children really needed, or so the thinking ran. Once again, the shadow between socialist Utopianism and the realities of human needs proved longer than expected. Facilities were often overcrowded, understaffed, and characterized by shortages in food and clothing. Discipline was either severe or lacking altogether. So bad were conditions in these homes that many children preferred life on the streets. "I declare without exaggeration that we have, not children's homes, but children's cemeteries and cesspools in the literal sense of the words," wrote one observer.[4]

Life on the street invariably meant a life of crime, usually petty theft. The prevailing attitude toward *besprizornye* was one of hostility. A 1935 law decreed that when these children were arrested, they were to be tried as adults. By 1937, some 65 percent of *besprizornye* between the ages of twelve and fifteen who ran afoul of the law were sent to labor camps. Others were simply shot, particularly if they were found to have venereal diseases.[5]

The Soviets were right about one thing, though. The state-run system of children's homes did produce children who were useful to at least one government agency: the KGB. "According to scattered claims," wrote historian Alan Ball, "'state children' also gained employment in the secret police, thereby exchanging the roles of defendant and inmate for those of guard, interrogator and executioner . . .

They purportedly carried out the security force's commands without hesitation."[6]

For a time, Lunacharsky's views fell out of favor. They were replaced by those of Anton Makarenko, who was, like Lunacharsky, a Ukrainian. A Stalinist educational theorist, Makarenko differed with Lunacharsky in style, not substance. He, too, saw it as the chief end of man to serve and worship the Soviet state forever. Experience taught him, however, that this could not be brought about by the state alone. Families would be needed, but a new Soviet-centric family, not the traditional pre-1917 version. Whatever his reputation now, it should not be forgotten that Makarenko was no less hostile to the family than Lunacharsky was.[7] "Family" was redefined in much the same way that "marriage" is being redefined in our own time. Traditional structures and methods were replaced with new Soviet ones. No longer, he said, were parental values and authority to be derived from the Church and the Ten Commandments (again, like Lunacharsky, whose first move was to close church schools). "Now we do not deceive children," Makarenko said.[8] Parents and schools were to model their structures on the Soviet state itself. The whole progression—authoritarian family, authoritarian school, and life as an adult in an authoritarian state—was designed to inculcate discipline and unquestioning loyalty.[9] But not a loyalty to schoolmasters or parents; loyalty was to be to the state alone. Indeed, children were encouraged to report politically incorrect teachers or relatives. Thus tyranny was extended to every aspect of Soviet life.

And what was the model for Makarenko's theories? The army and the Soviet system of labor camps. These should not be confused with the Head Start Program. Yes, as American mothers were raising a generation of children according to the instant-gratification precepts of Dr. Benjamin Spock, Russian and Ukrainian schools and orphanages were using the Red Army manual for drill and discipline. Orphanages provided the ideal control group for Makarenko's experiments in social engineering, just as Lunacharsky's had done.

Predictably, the Soviet Union institutionalized Makarenko's idiocy, making his theories the guiding principles of the educational system. According to Human Rights Watch: "Soviet-era policies and practices persist in Russian institutions. Renowned for its centralized control, the sprawling system of internaty [orphanages] for abandoned children was inspired by Soviet philosophy favoring collective organization over individual care, and the idea that the state could replace the family. Regimentation and discipline were integral to this philosophy, and restricted access to the institutions apparently permitted the director and staff to operate with impunity."[10]

As with most evil ideas that take root, not all of those ascribed to Lunacharsky and Makarenko are nonsensical, hence their appeal and longevity. These men were, for instance, certainly correct to emphasize a child's need for structure, purpose, discipline, and self-respect. As atheists and strict materialists, however, they denied utterly that man had a spiritual dimension. This led them to address human needs as one might treat those of a plant: give it water, food, and sunlight, and—*poof!* You have a healthy, productive yield.

Unfortunately, Lunacharsky's theories would be revived after Stalin's death. Both men enjoy a certain posthumous celebrity in the former Soviet Union, where the orphanages bear their indelible imprint.

True, orphanages in Russia and Ukraine are not as squalid today as they once were, but that is hardly a mark in the government's favor, since improvements are largely due to international aid. In some instances, Ukrainian orphanages receive more funding from sources outside of Ukraine than from agencies within it.[11] In both countries the governments are satisfied to allow foreign NGOs to provide what the governments will not; such is the prevailing attitude toward their own sick and fatherless. Of those foreign organizations meeting the needs of these children, many are Christian.[12] I remind you of the short-term missionaries who built playgrounds and improved the facilities at #17. This is just a microcosm of the work being done by thousands of short-term missionaries all over the former East Bloc. But it is not enough. Children still languish in conditions that would horrify most Americans.

As for orphanage "graduates," the situation has hardly improved from the Stalinist era. According to the Russian Interior Ministry's own estimates, 30 percent will enter a life of crime, 40 percent will become addicted to drugs or alcohol, 60 percent of girls will become prostitutes, and 10 percent of these children will commit suicide.[13] What of the nongraduates? In Ukraine, 30 percent of those with severe disabilities will be dead by the age of eighteen.[14] In some cases, mortality rates are said to run three and even four times as high as those of the general population.[15] So much for socialist Utopia.

Of course, no one really knows what happens to these children. Since they often disappear after they are ejected into the streets, such statistics can only be guesswork. And the government is less than forthcoming with the data, but if they will admit this much, the real figures are probably higher. I am reminded of a line from Pasternak's *Doctor Zhivago*: "One day Lara went out and did not come back. She must have been arrested in the street, as so often happened in those days, and she died or vanished somewhere, forgotten as a nameless number on a list which later was mislaid."[16]

TEN

What Have We Become?

*"Do not take advantage of a widow or an orphan.
If you do and they cry out to me, I will certainly
hear their cry. My anger will be aroused, and I
will kill you."*

—Exodus 22:22–24 NIV

AS OUR TIME IN UKRAINE DRAGGED ON, WE SETTLED INTO A
routine. I found a café within walking distance of our
apartment and spent the mornings there, working on my
laptop. Interruptions were few since I didn't know anyone. Christopher and Zachary were homeschooled, so it
was possible for them to continue their education from the
apartment. Lauri would set them to work in the morning
and check on them at regular intervals while she cleaned,
did the laundry, and prepared our meals.

With their usual sports activities on hold until we got
back home, Chris, Zach, and I would go for long walks
in the afternoons, and that, I can tell you, was a sport in
itself. Ukrainian sidewalks contain every sort of obstacle,

the greatest of these being manholes, as they are frequently covered improperly or not covered at all. To call the entry points to this city's sewer system manholes is utterly inadequate. *Man-whole* is getting closer to the mark, but even that doesn't quite capture it, as they are far less discriminating. Indeed, men, women, children, farm animals, automobiles—darn well everything has been known to disappear into their depths at one time or another.

And then there was the nature of public interaction. Generally speaking, it was harsh and lacking in civility. Being Americans—no, worse, Americans from *the South*—we were ill equipped for what was sometimes a kill-or-be-killed atmosphere. It is a bit like answering the phone only to discover that it's a telemarketer. The sensible thing to do is hang up. Of course, many Americans, in an effort to be polite, have trouble getting off the phone. Imagine a whole society preying on you like that. You now have a glimpse of public life in a former communist country. Courtesy will get you nowhere.

Occasionally this led to comical episodes of an almost slapstick nature. Stopping in at McDonald's one day, I gave Zachary money for ice cream. As he made his way to the counter, I watched with morbid fascination. The place was packed, and he had little notion of what awaited him. And of course, I did not tell him. He politely stood in what he thought was a line. You know, where the cashier says, "Can I help someone?" and you say to the woman next to you, "Go ahead; you were here before me," and you wave her in front and then wait your turn? No such considerations were at work in Ukraine, but Zachary did not yet know it.

Twice he stepped forward to place his order, and twice he was unceremoniously pushed aside by others who had just walked though the door. He stepped back, disconcerted. Turning to me, he held up his hands and mouthed, "Did you see that?" I shrugged as if equally confused.

Squaring his shoulders to the counter, he surged forward with determination when the next cashier became available. I could tell that it required some effort for him to put aside good manners, but a hot fudge sundae proved to be sufficient motivation. Though an amusing anecdote, it is instructive of what happens to civility in this kind of world. It is simply stamped out.

Most of the time, however, there was nothing remotely amusing about the experience. To board a tram or a bus was to invite harassment from thick-necked public officials or thugs—it was hard to tell the difference—who flashed badges and demanded money. These encounters were invariably tense, and until somebody paid, no one was permitted to disembark. Customs and border officials were much the same, rummaging through luggage, purses, and wallets. Rumor has it that police profit from the criminal activities of the *besprizornye* who can be seen restlessly roaming the city streets at any hour.

Observing that I had put my backpack down beside my chair in a reasonably nice restaurant, Viktor warned, "You better put your leg through one of the arm straps."

"What?" I protested. "In here?"

He lifted the tablecloth slightly to show me that he had done precisely as he now advised. "Yes. I would if I wanted to keep that backpack."

No sooner had I done so when a little gang of shabby boys burst forth from the street and, before the security guard could impede them, made their way from table to table, begging. Women picked up their purses and held them. Men did likewise with briefcases and shoulder bags. Veterans, these people knew what the boys were after. And yet I was deeply moved by the sight of this careworn and hollow-cheeked retinue. Who among us would not steal in similar circumstances? Public life in that part of the world is characterized by hardness and indifference. The government set the standard: *those sitting above can easily spit on those below.*

AFTER NUMEROUS DELAYS, WE BEGAN TO SEE OUR FIRST real progress toward adopting Sasha since arriving in Odessa. We were now permitted to officially accept the "referral for adoption." This involves a piece of paper with signatures and seals from an assortment of adoption officials. The document is vital. Obtaining it requires a series of frustrating and largely unnecessary steps. No court date can be scheduled without it, and the court appearance is the ultimate goal. It decides the adoption.

First, we waited for a week. We made many calls to

expedite this process, but we might as well have called the number for the local time and temperature for all the good it did. Then we were told that we had to take the AI to the orphanage. (Yes, you bear the responsibility and expense of getting government officials to the places where they are supposed to be, and then you have to bribe them to do what they are supposed to do.) Excited to finally be doing something, we went to her home as directed. She wasn't ready, so we waited in the car. Once at the orphanage, the AI and the orphanage director passed papers back and forth the way Gorbachev and Reagan might have done at Reykjavík. Lauri and I waited in the car. From there, our facilitator went to make copies. We waited in the car. Then it was back to the orphanage to get more signatures. We waited. At this point, I began to detect a pattern and passed the time poking around the orphanage.

Driving the AI back to her office, I wondered at the life she led. The ring, or, more accurately, the *sing* of her cell phone interrupted my musings. The ringtone was Celine Dion's "My Heart Will Go On," the theme song for the hit movie *Titanic*. Here was an insight. At heart, the AI was a romantic. She had probably watched that movie a dozen times with a box of tissues on her lap. Either that or the song reminded her of another cheery Ukrainian proverb, like "For big ships, big icebergs." She seemed to be in high spirits. Apparently, good bribes have that effect. She turned, briefly surveyed Lauri and me as we sat in the backseat, and then spoke to Viktor.

"She says that Sasha looks like one of your biological children," Viktor translated, looking at me in his rearview mirror. I wasn't sure of her motivation for saying it, but I figured she was trying to be cordial. While our monetary exchanges had never been direct, she undoubtedly sensed my simmering hostility. She smiled warmly and then spoke to Viktor again.

Viktor looked amused. "She says that you look Ukrainian."

"Really?" I wondered if it was my facial features or simply because I was, at that moment, wearing the unofficial colors of Ukraine: black and black on a field of black.

Back at her office, it felt as though something momentous had been accomplished. We had two important documents: one initiating the adoption and the other a report from the Odessa Police, stating that the whereabouts of Sasha's biological mother were unknown. The first document was routine. The second was an insurance policy. We wanted to have it on hand in case we encountered a surly judge in our court hearing. A judge might require us to track down the biological mother, who had not appeared on anyone's radar for more than a decade. Indeed, her very name and existence were mere conjecture, so a court order of this type would likely end our bid to adopt Sasha.

And surly judges are not unknown in Ukraine. The Mortons, the American couple accused of wanting to adopt so they could harvest the adopted child's organs, found themselves at the mercy of just such a magistrate. Hours before their court appointment, the judge abruptly canceled the hearing. He knew very well that the Mortons had planned to fly home to Pennsylvania to sit out the ten-day waiting period that follows the hearing. They were understandably demoralized. Waiting meant more money, penalties from the airlines for changing their flight schedule, their employers' displeasure, and above all, uncertainty about the adoption itself. Had it all been in vain?

I nonetheless remained an optimistic American. Our experience would be different. I mean, what were the odds that we both had corrupt judges? Better than I knew, I'm afraid.

WITH OUR COURT DATE SCHEDULED, WE BOOKED FLIGHTS HOME for the mandatory ten-day waiting period. I had work that required my attention back in the States, and everyone was growing a bit weary of Ukraine. Even so, our family was excited. We were getting closer to the end. We were closer to taking Sasha home with us.

Or so we thought.

The next day, Arkady and I went to see the AI for a routine visit while Viktor attended to other business. Returning to the car, I could tell from Arkady's forlorn expression that I would not like what he had to say.

"The judge cannot make the court appearance on Tuesday," he said, collapsing into the car seat and slamming the door.

"What? Didn't she set the date in the first place?"

Arkady's face said what I already knew: *That is beside the point. This is all part of the game. Play the game!*

As we drove out of the parking lot, Arkady slid a CD into his stereo. "One of your American Christians gave this to me." He smiled broadly, trying to cheer me up. "Perhaps you will like it?" Moments later the words rang out:

> *What have we become?*
> *Tell me, where are the righteous ones?*

"Arkady, she wants another bribe, doesn't she?" I asked, suppressing a rising anger.

> *What have we become?*
> *In a world degenerating . . .*

He lifted his hands slightly in a gesture of agreement, but without letting go of the steering wheel. "Of course," he said, his smile never dimming.

> *What about mercy, compassion, and selflessness?*

Momentarily, I became aware of the song's lyrics. *Degenerating, indeed*, I thought. I felt a great sadness that had nothing to do with flights, home, or the inconvenience and expense this would surely cause us. Rather, my spirit was grieved to discover a system so rotten that it actively conspired against "the least of these." (See Matthew 25:31–46.)

The corruption and apathy of the government's practices made the Ulysses Grant administration look like one long seminar in good ethics.

A light rain began to fall, darkening the dust-covered sidewalks and dirty pre-Revolution architecture that lined the road between the orphanage and the adoption inspector's office. The effect was that of a city in mourning. It was as if the buildings themselves had heard and absorbed the cries of Ukraine's forgotten children and, after decades of silence, now grieved for them. As I stared out the window at nothing in particular, Exodus 22:22–24 came to mind: "Do not take advantage of a widow or an orphan. If you do and they cry out to me, I will certainly hear their cry. My anger will be aroused, and I will kill you" (NIV).

I concluded that the people in this diabolical bureaucracy did not fear God. They should. God is a God of grace, to be sure, but he is also a God of justice. And a society that has no regard for its children is a society that has no regard for its future—in this world or the next.

ELEVEN

Life Is Cheap

What is hell? I maintain that it is the suffering of being unable to love.

—FYODOR DOSTOEVSKY[1]

IT HAPPENED ON FRIDAY MORNING, APRIL 26, 1986, AT 1:23 A.M. Although there was no word from the government of the disaster, within days a nuclear power station in Sweden detected abnormally high levels of radiation in winds coming from the east. A nuclear event one hundred times greater than Hiroshima and Nagasaki combined had occurred somewhere inside the Soviet Union. There had been a meltdown at reactor number four at a place till then known only to a few specialists—*Chernobyl*.

Firefighters sent to the scene on the night of the disaster were given no protective clothing. Instead, they used the same techniques and equipment to deal with the fire as they would any other, spraying water onto the building and shoveling dirt through the collapsed ceiling of the ruptured reactor. Soon townspeople were experiencing nausea, headaches, and slurred speech, while others became comatose. Still, the government gave no official announcement or acknowledgment of the event. By Sunday, residents of the nearby town of Pripyat were quietly evacuated. Sixty miles to the south, people in Kiev, unaware of the catastrophe, celebrated May Day as planned. The more observant among them knew, however, that something had happened. In parts of the city, ash and a kind of sticky, bloblike substance fell from the sky, and perhaps most telling of all, the party apparatchiki were leaving Kiev—with their families.

Realizing that the secret could no longer be contained, the government issued an announcement of the accident but made no mention of health risks and buried the report in a nightly news program. It was enough. Kievans crowded roads leaving the city, only to find machine gun–wielding militia blocking their exodus. All those without approved passes were directed back to Kiev. Meanwhile, at Chernobyl itself, employees continued to work in and around the reactor without protective gear. It was simply a fire, they were told. No mention was made of radiation.

Precisely how many lives were needlessly lost as a result of the Chernobyl meltdown and the government's response is a mystery. Figures have been deliberately muddled, falsified, or destroyed. According to a 2005 World Health Organization study, 56 people died in the blast or immediate aftermath, mostly firefighters and plant personnel, with possibly another 4,000 dying in subsequent months. This does not include birth defects or the 600,000 people who have suffered from cancer and leukemia or will die prematurely as a result of their exposure to high levels of radiation. Journalist Anna Reid, who has written extensively on the subject, has called Chernobyl "a saga of technical incompetence and irresponsibility, of bureaucratic sloth, mendacity and plain contempt for human life."[2]

One trip to the Chernobyl Museum in Kiev and you understand precisely what Reid is talking about. As a facility, the museum is unimpressive. There is no IMAX theatre, no models simulating the explosion and subsequent fallout, and no food court. Instead, there are simply display cases filled with official memoranda, letters, and newspaper clippings. As you exit the museum, you will see a wall covered with photographs of children—all of whom have suffered birth defects as a result of Chernobyl. Their faces haunt me.

Today, in spite of government promises, thousands of people are still living inside the evacuation zone, an area estimated to be unsafe for another two hundred years. Operations at the plant continued until 2000 and only then ended due to international pressure. Seventy-five years of communist rule—some say the communists *still* rule— were not without effect.

In communist countries—or, as in the case of Ukraine, former communist countries—life is cheap. As one American missionary put it to me, "It is not a place to be old, sick, or needy." No it is not. It is said that great suffering produces great art and literature. Not in Ukraine. There, suffering has just produced more suffering. Take World War II as an example. It is estimated that anywhere between 7.5 million and 11 million Ukrainians died. That was roughly one-third of Ukraine's population at the time. The American death toll numbered about 400,000.

On my first trip to Kiev some years ago, I made it a point to travel to the outskirts of the city to a place called Babyn Yar. There's not much there. Thank God. In this ravine, *Einsatzgruppen SS* and Ukrainian police murdered some 100,000 people during the Nazi occupation. It is the largest single massacre in history. Whatever the horrors we have experienced in our history, we have no equivalent to this. Thank God again. It was, I thought, revealing that almost none of the locals could tell me where Babyn Yar was. Few had even heard of it. After all, to them it was just another place in a long list of sorrowful and tragic places. Is it any wonder that such a culture should produce proverbs of hopelessness and regard human life as less than sacred?

All of this was reflected in people's attitudes toward the poor, the sick, and the orphaned. Walking the streets of Odessa each day, I passed beggars of a type not often seen in the West. These were not the able-bodied, well-fed sorts seen in America. They were amputees, old-age pensioners, and children. The image of one man is forever etched in my memory. More than legless, his body appeared to be missing from his navel down. Honestly, I don't know how he was alive. He moved around the streets on his hands. Finding a suitable spot for his trade, he would carefully arrange a dirty cloth on the ground and then rest his torso on it. Another man, a midget, worked the same territory. People, usually teens, openly jeered at them. Old men and women moved up and down city streets as supplicants, hoping for spare change or a bit of food from those dining in fashionable restaurants and at sidewalk cafés. And these are not all poor city streets, mind you. Ferraris, Lamborghinis, Porsches, and other supercars are so common that it's like watching an episode of *Top Gear*. At Odessa's ports, impressive yachts come and go regularly. Such displays of wealth and power are extravagant in the best of circumstances, but they become crass and arrogant when you consider that the children in Orphanage #17, who reside in the same city, do not even have toilet paper— *toilet paper.*

The destitute can be seen all over the former Soviet Union. That is, when the police do not chase them away. Traveling in Russia some years ago, I was in St. Petersburg. As I stood in front of St. Isaac's Cathedral, a woman of at least seventy offered to sell me postcards. She fanned them out in her gnarled hands.

"You buy?"

"Give her nothing," my Russian guide instructed before barking at the woman. I didn't want any postcards, but something in her deeply furrowed face spoke of desperation. I reached in my pocket for some money and gave it to her. She handed me the whole stack of tattered souvenir photographs.

"No, I just want *one*," I said. I held up a finger to make my meaning clear. Selecting a postcard, I gave the rest back to her. If I took them all, she would have nothing left to sell. My guide looked exasperated.

Beneath the scarf that covered the old woman's head, tears began to flow. Taking my hand, she kissed it and then walked away, her body bowed from age and a lifetime of worries. I had done nothing. It had cost me nothing.

I turned to my guide. "Why did you tell me not to give her anything?"

"Because these beggars sit out in front of tourist attractions, waiting for Americans like you." She was annoyed that I had not heeded her counsel. "They are here to *take advantage* of you."

"Are you saying that she is not really poor? That she's just pretending to be poor?"

"No, I am not saying that." She gave a shrug. "She's an old-age pensioner. What the government gives her is not enough to survive on. I'll guarantee you that she is going to buy bread with what you just gave her. It will feed her for a week."

That sort of indifference, jarring to me at the time, is characteristic of much of the former East Bloc. I well understood why people might ignore those for whom panhandling had become a means of dishonest gain. I recollect walking down Broad Street in Oxford, England, when my colleague spotted a woman sitting on the sidewalk, holding a baby and the ubiquitous "Will work for food" sign. He stepped into a fast-food restaurant; purchased a burger, fries, and drink; and brought them out to her. She threw the sack of food back at him. She wanted money, not work or food. More recently, in America, I saw a man standing outside of Wrigley Field with a cardboard sign reading, "I can't lie. I just want a cold beer." At least he was honest.

In Ukraine, however, there is little material assistance to be found. Government aid is inadequate. There are few shelters. Street children crowd into twenty-four-hour Internet cafés, having nowhere else to go. And Christian charity, the backbone of benevolence in any society, is often lacking because authentic Christians are but a tiny minority of the population. Consequently, the attitudes with which we were confronted in the orphanages and the government that ran them were merely reflective of those in the larger culture.

Learning that I was in their country, a small group of academics asked me to come and speak on the religious climate in America. My lecture over, I was ready to take questions. A hand went up and a woman asked, "Why are you in Ukraine?"

"My wife and I are here finalizing the adoption of a ten-year-old girl." I assumed that would be the end of the matter and we would move to the topic of my address. I was wrong.

A man asked, "Why would you want to adopt?" Frankly,

this seemed a silly question. Aren't the reasons for adoption self-evident? A couple loves children; a child needs a home and a family; the family hopes to make a difference in the life of another human being, and so on. I then realized that his question was shared by the whole room. *Why adopt? Who would want to do that?*

"You do understand that orphans are *different*, don't you?" a woman at the back of the room put in.

"*Besprizornye*," added another. There it was again. That heavy, damning word. Whatever its literal meaning in Russian—"ones without oversight" or "those without supervision"—the tone and the context in which they used it implied another species, as if we were speaking of stray dogs or cats instead of children.

The rest of the question-and-answer period became a referendum on adoption, and my party did not win. There was little sympathy with my views. It wasn't just that my audience didn't want to adopt children. It was a great deal more than that. The whole concept was anathema to most of them. That, of course, is because the concept *is* anathema to a culture not heavily influenced by a Christian worldview. As has already been demonstrated, atheists don't do benevolence. Adoption facilitators will tell you that very few Ukrainians or Russians adopt or volunteer their time for these abandoned children. And there is little help being offered from the Islamic world, countries where the slave trade continues to thrive. No, as with most aid, most adoptions are to parents from Western countries, overwhelmingly, to those from the United States. According to the U.S. State Department, "Since 1986, American parents have adopted nearly 84,000 children from Eastern Europe and countries of the former Soviet Union."[3] Why do Americans do it? It is a result of Christianity's influence in America. It is the grace effect.

TWELVE

The Purchase of a Soul

"Love is the foolishness of men and the wisdom of God."

—FROM VICTOR HUGO'S *LES MISÉRABLES*[1]

TOILETS AREN'T THE ONLY THINGS THAT STINK IN UKRAINE. CALL it what you like: an expediting fee, a gift, an administrative contribution—they are all euphemisms for bribery, and the effect is the same: *children are for sale in Ukraine.* "It is the way in Ukraine," people will say. Translation: It is just part of the culture. I have heard people who should know better say that. The British in India were told similar things about the Hindu practice of suttee, a ritual that involved burning a man's widow on his funeral pyre. The fact is, some cultural practices are damnable. The difference between a gift society and one that thrives on extortion is not as nuanced as some would have you believe.

Holding the levers of power are people who offer righteous expressions of concern for the children, and as evidence of their love and devotion, they cite their many laws, all there, they say, to protect the children from those who would exploit them. Recently, for example, the Russian government made much over the case of an eight-year-old boy who was returned to Moscow by his adoptive parent. The government assumed a sanctimonious air and used the episode to further restrict international adoptions. It is all phony.

The architects of this system are what Jesus might have called "whitewashed tombs" (see Matthew 23:27). No wonder Gregory Potemkin is one of Ukraine's favorite sons. Inventor of the "Potemkin village," he was once Ukraine's shammer-in-chief, creating a world of illusion and collusion where nothing was as it seemed. Dante was right. Corrupt politicians do belong in (at least) the eighth circle of hell. Dante, I am convinced, had adopted a child from Ukraine.

An American missionary in Odessa offered this insight: "Remember, in dealing with the Ukrainian government, it's never about the 'thing,' whatever the 'thing' is. It's all about power." I will go one further: it's about the powers of darkness. Satan, the architect of this evil system, is vying for the souls of these children. And the closer we got to our goal, the more forces it seemed he brought to bear.

International adoption is a scary thing for a child above the age of toddlerhood. This is especially true if the child has never known anything beyond orphanage life. Think about it—he is going to live with a family whose language he cannot speak, in a country where he has never been, and in circumstances he has not known. Satan plays on these fears skillfully, and he does it through other children in the orphanage and through some of the adoption officials. The wiser and more compassionate among officials know that adoption is the best thing for these children, but for others, to hear that a child prefers the orphanage to adoption is music to their ears. A salve, perhaps, to a guilty conscience, it confirms them in their opinion that they *really are* running a good operation, after all. I also think there's no small measure of national pride at stake. For a child to choose the orphanage over adoption is to choose Ukrainians over Americans.

And that's just it—the child is put in the position of choosing. He must write a letter stating that he wants to be adopted and then, at the court appearance, must say so verbally. The system allows the child's future to be determined by the *whims* of a child—*or do they*?

In one recent court hearing, some would-be parents were stunned when the girl they planned to adopt told the judge she did not want to be adopted. Fortunately, the orphanage director had her best interests in mind and, conducting her own investigation, discovered that one of the little girl's teachers was pressuring her to say no. Evidently, the teachers are paid according to the number of pupils they have. Every adoption means less money in their paychecks. If true, this is yet one more way the system conspires against these orphans and their futures.

ANOTHER BRIBE TO THE AI, AND WE WERE BACK ON SCHEDULE with our Tuesday court date. If all went well there, the clock would start on the mandatory ten-day waiting period. Then, God willing, Sasha would become a member of our family. The purpose of the waiting period is to allow any relatives to come forward to contest the adoption. This was just adding insult to injury. Sasha, almost eleven, had been in one orphanage or another since birth. In a sense, her whole life—roughly four thousand days—had been a waiting period. No one had claimed her. Still, the government, ever conscientious, wanted to make sure these nonexistent family members got ten more days.

The day of our court appearance began, predictably, with another threat of postponement. The AI had already been paid, so it was only fitting that the judge should now notice a conflict on her calendar. Even so, we managed to appease her and maintain our appointed time.

Arriving at the courthouse, Lauri and I waited for the AI, the orphanage director, and Sasha. Once again, it was our responsibility to transport everyone, so we had to send taxis to get them. Inside the courthouse, people thronged the entryway and corridors. As in every other government building we had seen, the number of places to sit was wholly inadequate, so Lauri and I opted for a little grassy spot outside on the courthouse grounds. Spirits high, we were cautiously optimistic that this day would see us clear a major legal hurdle.

At long last, Sasha, the AI, and the orphanage director arrived. Sasha appeared to be wearing her best clothes: a denim jumper, a white shirt with frills at the neck and wrists, yellow stockings, and red Puma tennis shoes. It was an incongruous combination, but we thought she looked adorable. Our appointed time came and went. We all sat impatiently. Lauri tried to keep Sasha busy with games while I paced the halls and observed what proceedings I could.

Finally, we were summoned. It was not what I expected. Rather than a courtroom, we were called into the judge's office. A room about ten by ten, it was already full of people whose function was never made clear to us. We were told to sit down and then were read, in Russian, our rights. Most curious of all was the judge. A twentysomething bleach blonde, she wore a skintight miniskirt and tottered around on five-inch stilettos. She looked like the Ukrainian version of Christina Aguilera. Lauri turned to me, her eyebrow raised in mock suspicion. I whispered to her that I had never seen a judge like *that* before. Apparently, she was a typical female representative of that office. So much so that the Ukrainian government later issued a dress code.[2]

The office was decorated with Russian Orthodox icons, a statue of Lady Justice holding her sword and scales, and photos of schnauzers. It was as though Alabama and Ukraine had met somewhere in the Twilight Zone, and, given that we were Alabamans in Ukraine, it seemed fitting. For a time, we were merely spectators. Documents were passed between the various parties as the judge presided. Viktor appeared nervous in her presence.

Wheeling in her chair to us, the judge, affecting a disinterested air, straightened the papers on her desk, then spoke in a soft, firm voice. Viktor, sitting to my left, elbowed me. "She's talking to you," he whispered. *"Stand up."* I sprang to my feet. Even without translation I could have guessed what she was saying.

"She wants to know how much money you make annually," Viktor relayed. "In square meters, how much living space is in your home?" she asked, looking down at her desk or out the window. These were questions we had answered several times before. It is kind of like one of those phone trees where an automated voice instructs you to "enter your ten-digit phone number" and then, when a human being comes on the line, you are asked to give your ten-digit phone number again. What was the point of keying it in the first time?

There was, however, one new question: "Will Sasha have her own room, or will she be required to share a room?" The judge, more condescending than ever, studied me and then looked at Sasha with a deep pathos. Lauri, perhaps sensing my contempt for this charade, gripped my forearm. She need not have worried. Like her, I had grown used to it. As such, I didn't say what I was thinking: *Does it matter? She is currently sleeping in a barracks! And we will love her.*

I smiled, certain that I had acted my part well. "Yes, she will have her own room."

Apparently satisfied with our answers, she turned her attention to the prosecutor, the AI, and the orphanage director, and then, finally, to Sasha.

If Sasha was intimidated by the proceedings, she didn't

show it. She smiled broadly throughout. The judge asked her if she wanted to be adopted.

"*Da*"—yes—she replied.

"Do you realize that you will be leaving the country?"

"*Da*."

"Do you know that you're going to a place where no one speaks Russian?"

"*Da*."

"Do you have any friends at the orphanage?"

"*Da*."

"Won't you miss them?"

"*Da*."

"Why do you want to be adopted by these people?"

These were very leading questions. Not what we had paid for in our dishonest magistrate. Lauri and I felt uneasy. She might have more honestly asked Sasha questions like, "Do you realize that you are leaving a hellhole?" and "Do you know that this country has failed you?" and "Are you aware of the fact that I will profit handsomely from this, whether you are adopted or not?"

It was a performance. Like so many other things in this country, it was a facade, a Potemkin village. The icons, the scales of justice, the expressions of concern—they were all a sham.

Suddenly, it was all over and Sasha was declared "Alexandra Lauren Taunton." Our facilitator whispered, "Say thank you to everyone." We did and, oddly, I meant it. This whole system works on your psyche like Stockholm syndrome. You're so grateful that they are letting you grovel and bribe them to do what anyone with a shred of conscience would feel legally and morally bound to do anyway, that you end up thanking them profusely for the opportunity to be abused.

The unlikely assemblage dispersed just as they had arrived: the judge exited the room as if parading down a catwalk; Viktor hailed a taxi for the AI, while Sasha and the orphanage director took another; and Lauri and I returned to our grassy haven outside.

Taking in the moment, Lauri and I looked at each other and smiled, both of us silently praising God for this victory. As we waited our turn to be ferried back to our apartment, I noticed a row of luxury cars parked in reserved spaces away from the rank-and-file Ladas. One car in particular caught my eye: a Mercedes, a big, expensive one. I waved Lauri over to inspect it.

"It belongs to the judge," I speculated.

Arkady arrived at just that moment to pick us up. "Yes," he said with that easy smile of his. "Americans bought her that car." So this was where she spent her bribe money. One look at her office showed that it clearly wasn't being spent on interior decoration. She could have bought most of that stuff from any Odessa street vendor selling *matryoshka* dolls, army surplus, and that sort of thing.

"How did a young woman like that become a judge?" I asked. Arkady raised his eyebrows and leaned in slightly.

"Do you need to ask, Larry?" He then gave me a manly

slap on the shoulder and guffawed. "No, actually"—he broke off his laughter and spoke solemnly—"her family is very powerful."

"Does she do a lot of adoption cases?"

"Yes, as well as other things, but adoptions are very profitable for her. Her regular salary combined with your fifteen-hundred-dollar 'gift' and that of many other Americans and she makes a very nice living, as you see." He gestured broadly toward the car as Vanna White might have done were it a grand prize. "But she is very corrupt even by our standards."

Wow. That's saying quite a lot, I thought.

Getting into his car, he turned to me gravely. Putting a finger to his temple as if it were a gun, he continued: "Shoot me in the head"—he fired the make-believe trigger—"and if you give her thirty thousand dollars, *you will walk.*" Arkady was whispering now. I didn't ask him if he was serious. His solemn expression made it all too clear that he was.

My cell phone rang.

"Larry?" It was Ivan, the facilitator of facilitators, calling from Kiev. "Congratulations! Viktor tells me that all went well today," he began. But I sensed there was more to his call than a simple desire to join the celebration. I was right.

"Larry, there is another matter that you must decide."

"Yes? What is it?" I braced.

"Sasha has some money . . ." He was speaking very slowly, deliberately.

"What? This is the first we have heard of it," I was genuinely surprised. "How much and who gave it to her?"

"The government puts a small sum of money into an account for orphans that they can access upon graduation," he explained. "It comes to about two hundred dollars a year. As her legal guardians, you can now withdraw it from the bank."

This seemed like good news. It would be the start of a savings account for Sasha. Or so I thought.

"The orphanage wants the money." Here was the crux of the matter. "You don't have to give it to them, but it is customary to make—"

"A *donation*," I said, concluding the sentence for him.

"Yes," he said. "Something like that."

"Why didn't they just help themselves to it?" I wondered aloud. "They were her legal guardians for years."

"Because the government won't let them. Only the child at graduation or other legal custodians."

Of course, I thought. *No one watches thieves as much as other thieves.*

After exploring our options, we decided that it was best to let them have the money. We weren't out of the country yet. Besides, they assured us that they would use the money to buy new clothes for the children. *Yeah, right.*

As I drove away from the courthouse, my thoughts returned to Sasha. This final theft notwithstanding, Lauri and I felt triumphant. Sasha was a Taunton. Whatever the cost in time, money, or frustration, a little girl was one step closer to crossing the Atlantic to a home and family in America. Lauri, Chris, Zach, Sasha, our facilitator, and I all went out for dinner to celebrate. Sasha, permitted to join us, wanted a Happy Meal. She seemed to grasp the significance of the moment. She practiced her name, badly butchering "Taunton."

LATER THAT EVENING, KNOWING THAT WE WERE NEARING THE mandatory ten-day waiting period, Lauri and I sat down with Sasha to tell her that we had to return to the United States. With court now behind us and pressing demands on the U.S. side of the Atlantic, we told her that we were going home, but at the end of the ten days, we would return for her. As Viktor interpreted, bewilderment seized Sasha. It seemed clear that she did not understand. Were we abandoning her? Would we ever come back? Why wasn't she going with us?

In that moment, the Upper Room discourse came to mind. There, Jesus spoke to his disciples of things to come. To them, however, he was speaking in riddles, talking about betrayal, death, joy, and a "Helper" whom he would send (John 16:7). "We do not know what he is talking about," they said to one another (v. 18). One thing Jesus said, however, the disciples understood well enough. They were alarmed by the revelation that he would be leaving them. Knowing that this upset them, Jesus offered words of comfort. "I go to prepare a place for you," he said (John 14:2). "I will not leave you as orphans; I will come to you" (v. 18).

"Sasha," I said, "We go to prepare a place for you. We will then come to get you." Lauri repeated the words. A few seconds later, the words translated, a smile crept across Sasha's face. We returned the smile reassuringly. She seemed relieved and even pleased by this additional information.

Perhaps my more cynical readers will think this a bit presumptuous on my part. After all, I am certainly not Jesus, and Alabama has never been confused with heaven. But the parallel between earthly and heavenly adoptions was not my contrivance. The Word of God, living and active, is powerful. Far from being outdated and irrelevant, it resonates with our experiences in everyday life. So much so that we find parallels for heavenly things in earthly things—slavery mirrors our bondage in sin; marriage, our relationship with Christ—indeed, such are the sacraments themselves. But of the many spiritual truths reflected in this life, adoption is among the most profound. In redeeming us, Jesus Christ made us his own children, thus we are heirs to a great promise and a great hope. Still, we are often anxious or afraid because we cannot fully grasp the richness of what our future holds.

And Sasha couldn't either. Not really. She had been told that we would give her a better life, and, *on faith*, she had accepted that. But she could no more comprehend what that meant than we can fathom what heaven is. "Better" is a concept we can grasp, but the full measure of how a given thing is so, lies well beyond our mental abilities, as we have no basis for comparison. *"Heaven is like a perfect day at the beach"*—silly, right? Every reference point is inadequate to anyone who has not experienced the thing being described. Similarly, to tell Sasha that her new life would be better because she would have a family who loves and cares for her may have conjured warm and fuzzy feelings, but it was an abstract concept because the word *family* had practically no context in her world.

This was brought powerfully home to us one day as we walked together along one of Odessa's broad boulevards. Lauri told Sasha that she would now have cousins in addition to brothers. Viktor translated, but Sasha looked puzzled. Perceptively, Lauri told Viktor to ask Sasha if she knew what cousins were. She did not. How one family member was related to another remained largely an abstraction to her. But Sasha's life was about to change. If no one stepped forward to challenge the adoption during the waiting period, Sasha would soon have a family of her own—brothers, parents, grandparents, and all. I am reminded of a line from the brilliant musical version of Victor Hugo's *Les Misérables*, where Jean Valjean purchases the freedom of the orphan Cosette: *Come, Cosette. Say Good-bye. Let us seek out some friendlier sky.*

THIRTEEN

Mountains to Climb

*A glimpse is not a vision. But to a man on a
mountain road by night, a glimpse of the next
three feet of road may matter more than a vision
of the horizon.*

—C. S. LEWIS

OF THE MANY OBSTACLES ENCOUNTERED ON THE WAY TO AN
international adoption, most are faced exclusively by the
adopting parents. Finding financial resources, home inspections, interviews, committing the necessary time to travel,
dealing with corrupt politicians, bureaucratic hassles, and
so on—none of these require anything from the child you
hope to adopt. But make no mistake about it: the child faces
a plethora of difficulties equal to any of those confronting
the would-be parents—learning a new language, understanding a different culture, assimilating into a family, and
so on. One minor incident gave us a glimpse of the many
mountains Sasha must yet climb.

To facilitate Sasha's understanding of English, Lauri

and I decided to hire an English-speaking Ukrainian to tutor her. A girl named Tatyana, a language student at one of the universities in Odessa, was recommended to us. A no-nonsense young woman, she agreed to meet with Sasha for an hour's lesson each day at our apartment. On day two, Tatyana was displeased to discover that Sasha had not done her homework. Sasha's world was a mystery to the inexperienced and naive Tatyana. Sasha had never had any meaningful education, and while she spent her afternoons with us at the apartment, it was almost a certainty that she would get no assistance with homework at the orphanage. So, before her third lesson, I decided to sit down with Sasha to teach her the alphabet.

Not surprisingly, Sasha asserted her strong will and refused to cooperate. I sat at the kitchen table alone, inviting her to sit down with me. She stood in the corner, back turned and arms crossed, her whole bearing radiating defiance.

"Nyet," she said. Speaking through our ever-present Ukrainian translator, Viktor, she declared her inability to learn the language. "I cannot do it. It is too much to learn." Still, I tried, Viktor faithfully translating my many entreaties. "Nyet," was the inevitable response.

A former educator myself, I knew the difference between defiance that is motivated by disrespect and defiance that is born of a lack of confidence. I have taught many a sassy child, and Sasha's resistance, I was confident, had much more to do with the latter than the former. Sasha's education had been badly neglected, like so much else in her life.

"Sasha doesn't do anything she does not want to do," one of her teachers told us with a dismissive air. How sad. A ten-year-old, it seems, had defeated an adult whose charge it was to teach children. No willful child left to make his own decisions would ever brush his teeth, eat veggies, or go to bed at a proper time, much less choose to be educated. Some things must not be presented as options.

Sasha still stood with her back to me. Seeing that a frontal approach would not be successful, I changed tactics.

"Viktor, tell her that is fine. The boys and I will do it without her." I then began to sing the alphabet song. Repeatedly, I sang it. Sasha stood like a monument in the corner. Our two boys, Christopher and Zachary, trusting that this was not sheer madness, dutifully sang with me.

" . . . Now I know my ABCs; won't you sing along with me?" I ended the song as a plea. Viktor translated.

"Nyet." If anything, her scowl was more severe.

"Boys, let's play 'Alphabet Uno.'"

What? their faces asked. I was making this up as I went along. The boys had just taught Sasha how to play Uno, and she loved the game.

"Just follow my lead, boys," I said under my breath. They looked at each other, confused, but played along.

"Draw two, Zach. That means you have to sing the song twice," I said. Ever my faithful conspirators, Zachary and Christopher performed beautifully.

"Look, a 7, Chris! You have to name the seventh letter of the alphabet."

"It's . . . let's see . . ." Chris pretended to concentrate. "G!"

A Wild card was played. "That means we all have to sing the alphabet song!" For a solid half hour we sang and played our silly game.

"Larry! Enough already! She's not going to do it!" Understandably, my wife, Lauri, had had enough.

"Be patient," I whispered. Why I whispered, I do not know. Sasha could not, after all, understand a word of English.

For teachers and parents, once the battle is engaged, *you must win*. You must establish that of the two wills, yours and the student's, yours is the strongest. Otherwise, the only lesson learned is to hold you in contempt. No, I was determined to break Sasha down. If she didn't learn the alphabet willingly, then she would learn it unwillingly, by perseveration.

And yet, in spite of her many refusals to participate, I knew that she wanted me to pursue her because she never left the room and she was clearly listening. Abandoning her corner, she crossed the kitchen and sat on the couch, her arms still folded in defiance, but this time only half-turned from us. *We were winning*.

"Sasha, can you sing the song?" I asked again.

"Nyet. It is too hard to memorize those letters," she declared emphatically through Viktor. "I cannot remember them."

I held up a Draw two card. "What is this?" I asked.

"It means you have to draw two from the pile," she said, bored.

"And this one?"

"Reverse. You have to change directions." Viktor sat forward, translating her words with more than usual interest.

"Really?" I asked. "Hmmm . . . How about this one?"

"It's a Draw four. You have to draw four if someone plays it against you." She lectured me as if I were a bit slow on the uptake. She named and explained them all—Skips, Wild cards, etc.—and how they are played.

"How do you know what these cards say, Sasha? You can't read the English printed on them, so how did you know?"

"I memorized them," she said, and then, briefly, our eyes met, exchanging a knowing look. Something was dawning on her.

"You *memorized* them? Well, now, that's interesting, isn't it?" I observed.

She well understood what I was implying. "That's different. It is a game. I cannot learn *Ahn-gleesky*." English. The last word was unmistakable, even in Russian. Although still defiant, Sasha's resolve was weakening. She had the look of someone who wanted to be upset but couldn't maintain the required intensity.

"Sasha, you *can* learn it. I think you're a smart little girl." At these words, she seemed to lift from her seat as though pricked with a needle. She swung her head around sharply and looked at me as if to determine whether I meant it or not. After a moment, she turned away again.

"I think you *want* to learn English because there is a lot you want to tell us, things you want us to know, but you can't communicate them to us," I continued.

"There is also a lot we want to tell you, but we can't. And I know that this frustrates you." Her shoulder remained turned to me, but that these words had struck something deep within her was clear. The room, previously chaotic, was silent. She seemed to be negotiating with herself.

Turning back to the table, the boys and I resumed our game of "Alphabet Uno," as it would become known. Quietly, Sasha moved to a nearby chair. With elbows on the table and her hands cradling her chin, she assumed an air of boredom. But when Christopher pretended to struggle, Sasha came to life and started singing softly.

"Viktor, please tell her to stop," I interrupted. "It is not her turn." Viktor dutifully translated, and Sasha stopped, puckering her lower lip and narrowing her eyes at me. It was all I could do not to laugh.

"Okay, Christopher, you may try again," I said. Chris resumed his singing, and she again sang with him.

"Viktor, please tell her to *stop*! It is not her turn," I repeated. Her face gave way to a broad smile.

"Sasha, you cannot help Christopher. It is cheating. You will have to wait your turn."

A third time she joined him, this time laughing. I feigned annoyance. For the next hour, we played alphabet games, all of them extemporized. In addition to Alphabet Uno, we made a hangman-like game and flash cards. She conquered them all.

"Sasha, I will hold up a card. For every letter you get right, you get a point," I explained. "For every one you get wrong, I get a point. At the end of the game, we will count them up to see who won. Understood?"

"*Da*," she said enthusiastically.

"Yes. Say *yes*," I demanded.

"Yahss!" She was kneeling on her chair at this point, leaning across the table toward me.

"I think I'm going to win. Because I don't think you can name them." This was meant to challenge her, and challenge her it did. Her competitive fires lit, she was now determined to beat me. And though she could not have known it, I wanted to be beaten.

"That's a *B*!" or "It is a *P*!" she would shout. Having won the letters, I placed them in her ever-growing pile.

"That's an *urrr*!"

"Nope," I said flatly. "It is an *R*." I placed that one in my pile.

Sasha turned to Viktor, rattled off something angrily in Russian, and then turned back to me, waiting for the translation. Viktor leaned forward, amused. "She says, 'That is what I said!'"

"No, you didn't," I told her. "You said 'urrr' and it is not an 'urrr.' It is an *R*." Practically growling, she watched my lips as I spoke, trying to pronounce the letters. And so we proceeded.

"Count the stacks!" she demanded at the end of the contest. There was no need, the outcome being obvious. "I won!" she declared with the zeal of a Super Bowl champion. No truer words were ever spoken. I hugged her and tousled her hair. There are times when teaching is tedious and unrewarding work. This, however, was not one of them.

Later that afternoon, Sasha went to the kitchen to help Lauri prepare dinner. She likes to do that, and Lauri loves the help. Standing at the counter, she began to hum and then to sing the alphabet song absentmindedly. Catching herself, she turned to see if I had heard her. Seeing my smile, she gave an embarrassed giggle and then returned to her assigned duties of chopping onions and tomatoes. It was a moment that I will always remember.

Perhaps this all seems like much ado about nothing. After all, she had only learned her ABCs. But ABCs were the least of what she learned that day. Sasha discovered that she *could* learn. This lesson, combined with the trust it had established, would serve her well in the months to come as she faced the challenges before her.

In his brilliant book *The Art of Teaching*, the late Gilbert Highet, for many years a classicist at Columbia University, says that a good teacher must have three qualities: he must know the subject, he must like the subject, and he must like his students. To this excellent list I make one addition: *he must believe in his students.* As we have seen, God manifests his grace to us in a variety of ways, not the least of which is family—and no one believes in a child's capacity to learn as much as her parents. Most of what a child learns comes via *informal* education; that is, those things that she learns from her parents or extended family. Whether it involves learning to tie a shoe or how to behave in polite society, parents are the key to a child's education because of their fundamental commitment to their children. Teachers, curricula, and schools of instruction come and go. If parents, the only constant throughout the entire process, are missing from the equation, the educational void it creates is incalculable.

Orphaned at birth and shuffled from one institution to another, Sasha's only constant had been instability. There had been no accountability and no one to believe in her. Because Sasha was willful and spirited, her teachers all too readily yielded when she resisted what little education she was offered. Worse yet, as a special-needs child, she had been consigned to an orphanage where the physically disabled were grouped with the mentally disabled. The void was considerable.

With a family to help her, however, the gap might be closed. She would need all the help we could offer and whatever reserves of determination she could summon if she was to scale the mountains that lay before her, *three feet at a time.*

FOURTEEN

Free at Last

Once more unto the breach, dear friends, once more!

—*HENRY V*, ACT 3, SCENE 1

BEFORE HIS HIGHLY PUBLICIZED ATTEMPT TO JUMP OVER thirteen Merlin buses at Wembley Stadium in London in 1975, American daredevil Evel Knievel met with broadcaster Frank Gifford in the press box for an interview. Gifford noticed that Knievel, studying the jump site on the field below, looked unsettled.

"What's wrong?" asked Gifford.

"I can't jump *that*," Knievel replied. "There are supposed to be thirteen buses down there. That's fourteen!"

"Perhaps you can get them to move one."

The daredevil shook his head. "You can't just start moving everything around. The calculations for a jump like this have to be precise. Besides, that would take hours."

Gifford understood. "Then I guess you are not going to make the jump." It was a statement, not a question.

Knievel was almost offended. "You can't do that. Ninety thousand people have paid to see me jump."

"What? You're going to do it anyway?" Gifford was dumbfounded.

"Of course. But I'll tell you right now, I'm going to land on that fourteenth bus."

Shortly thereafter, Knievel did precisely that, landing on the fourteenth bus at ninety miles per hour and breaking his pelvis in the process.

Some things are just stupid. Like Knievel's jump or Oliver Twist's "Please, sir, may I have some more?" they are an open invitation to misery. Many think that is what the adoption process is like. It is, they believe, a kind of Hotel California.[1] You hear it in the questions people will ask you. "Are you adopting?" the tone suggesting a question more like, "So, you enjoy self-flagellation?" One cannot blame them for wondering.

But adoption isn't like that. Oh, there were times when we felt as though we had just landed on the fourteenth bus. There were still others when, though I did not break my pelvis, I briefly considered breaking someone else's, so outrageous are the corruption and mistreatment of children.

Even so, it was worth every minute of it.

AFTER A BRIEF TRIP BACK TO BIRMINGHAM, WE RETURNED TO Odessa to finalize the adoption. So what was left? We had to get Sasha's new birth certificate, her Ukrainian tax ID (another bizarre law), her passport, and, finally, her visa from the United States government. God willing, Sasha would soon be traveling to her home in Birmingham, Alabama.

In spite of the things that remained undone, we looked with great anticipation to our first day back in Odessa. It was supposed to be Sasha's last at Orphanage #17.

"Where's Viktor?" Lauri asked impatiently.

"He won't be here until nine thirty," I said, trying to calm both our nerves. We had neither seen nor talked to Sasha since we had left Odessa ten days before—all efforts to do so were unsuccessful—so we didn't really know what to expect. I tried to imagine what she might be feeling or thinking. Did Sasha know that we were coming for her? Was she excited or frightened? Orphanage life had defined the boundaries of her existence. Now she would be leaving all of it behind.

My cell phone rang.

"Viktor?"

"Larry, I have some bad news," he began. I listened as Lauri tried to read my face and the intonation of my occasional "Uh-huh."

"Let me guess," she said as I hung up. "We can't get Sasha today?"

"I'm afraid not." We were back in Ukraine, all right. The AI, who must be present when the adopted child is withdrawn from the orphanage, suddenly declared that she was not available. Apparently *Titanic* was on television. Still, we managed to get word to Sasha that we were in the country and that we would soon be taking her away. She was, Viktor reported, bursting with excitement.

Two days later, we stood waiting impatiently, and, once again, things did not look promising. At 9 a.m. we were instructed to go to the local records office to obtain Sasha's new birth certificate. Upon arrival, we were told to come back at 11:00. We did. "Come back at 11:30," the reception-ist directed. We did. We waited some more. Then it was off to the regional records office to "authenticate the birth certificate." One might reasonably ask why the govern-ment must authenticate birth certificates that it has issued, but reason will get you nowhere in Ukraine. Besides, as it turned out, it didn't matter.

"Come back tomorrow," was the inevitable line. The woman who authenticates was on vacation. Authenticating, it seems, is tiring work, and one must take an occasional holiday to the Black Sea—wait a minute! Odessa is *on* the Black Sea . . .

Defeated, we then went to see the tax inspector (or TI for short). Sasha, according to Ukrainian law, was required to have a tax number before we could officially adopt her. Socialists, ever eager to tax the living and the dead, will pursue you even when you are no longer a citizen of the country in question. You really must applaud their efforts.

"I'll be down in a minute," the TI said. An hour passed. Making people wait is a petty expression of power, and every bureaucrat in the former East Bloc exercises it with relish.

Sitting in the taxi waiting, I again took note of the big,

expensive luxury sedans and SUVs in the parking lot. Every government building is lined with them. At that moment, the driver of a Mercedes gave a blast of his horn and, with an uncivilized gesture, indicated his desire for us to move out of his way. Our taxi driver, annoyed, grunted, pointed at the car, and said to me in a low voice, "Mafia." He said it before I could.

As if on cue, the TI, duly bribed, appeared and took our paper. "Come back at four," she said, and disappeared onto the street, tossing what looked like a buzzard-feather boa over her shoulder. I momentarily wished that it were of the constrictor type. The Holy Spirit interrupted my fantasy.

Then the AI called and (again) informed us that she could not go to the orphanage at the appointed time. Viktor, dangling the usual monetary incentives, managed to convince her to meet us later in the day. Another obstacle cleared, we made copies of the records—copies are required of everything—and hurried to the AI's office to pick her up. Once we were at the orphanage, the orphanage director, the AI, and the orphanage doctor all met with us. Papers were signed—lots and lots of papers.

But at the end of it all was little Sasha. With her hair braided around the periphery of her head, she stood beaming excitedly. "She looks like Princess Leia," Christopher would later observe. She stood holding something like a plastic grocery bag. It contained all of her worldly possessions.

As we made our way to the gate, children began to gather around Sasha, knowing the significance of the moment.

They said their good-byes and gave lots of hugs. When Lauri and I got into the taxi with her, Sasha's friends stood along the wrought-iron fence, their little hands waving.

"*Das vadanya*, Sasha!" Good-bye, Sasha.

She returned the waves enthusiastically as the car pulled away from the curb. I have never seen a child so excited. Not at Christmas, not on a birthday, not ever. Even the taxi driver was moved. Sasha began singing, choosing, appropriately, the alphabet song as her theme.

"Papa, I cannot remember my ABCs! Help me!" She was giddy.

For the first time, I noticed that the sky was as blue as I had ever seen. Not a cloud in sight. I do not say this for literary effect. It really was a perfect day. Sasha knew it, too, if only intuitively.

The taxi deposited us on a street near our apartment. Lauri and I walked the remaining block or so as Sasha broke into a sprint. Moments later, we could see her reaching the apartment, the door swinging open wide, and her eagerly embracing Christopher and Zachary. And that is how she would spend much of that evening—hugging everyone at regular intervals.

Lauri explained to Sasha some basic things about her new environment. Sasha smiled excitedly at the news that she would not be awakened early every morning for "exercises." Even more so when told that she would have a shower, with hot water, every day instead of once a week.

A shower, new pajamas, and lots of hugs later, she curled

up on the futon in the den, her temporary bed until we got back home. Within minutes she was asleep. I imagined sugar plum fairies dancing in her head. Sitting next to her, I couldn't help but wonder at the journey that had brought her to us— ten years and three orphanages. This was the first night *in her whole life* that she was not in one of them. The ransom paid, Sasha was free. Free, at least, to be what she might be without that system's gravitational force weighing down her life.

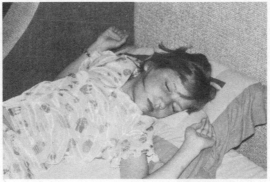

Photo by Christopher Taunton

Sasha's first night of freedom in the apartment in Odessa.

Did Sasha really understand the significance of it all? It is hard to say, but I think she did. Sasha understood that she now had brothers. She understood that she now had a mother and a father. That, more than anything else, excited her. "I prayed that God would let me have a family," she would later tell us. It seems her heavenly Father heard that prayer. "And [Jesus] said to them, 'Whoever receives this child in my name receives me, and whoever receives me receives him who sent me. For he who is least among you is the one who is great'" (Luke 9:48).

By the way, five months after the Wembley Stadium disaster, Knievel made another attempt at bus-jumping history. He again landed on the fourteenth bus, but this time managed to keep his balance and set a new world record. *"If at first you don't succeed . . ."*

FIFTEEN

The Importance of Identity

A good name is to be chosen rather than great
riches; and favor is better than silver or gold.

—Proverbs 22:1

UKRAINE'S MOST FAMOUS SON IS A MAN WHOSE REAL NAME IS
a matter of some dispute. It is not Leon Trotsky. We know
that dead maniac's real name was Lev Davidovich Bronstein.
It is neither Nikita Khrushchev nor Leonid Brezhnev, both
of whom were also Ukrainian. Besides, beyond the circles of
educated adults or those who lived through the Cold War,
few know anything about these communist icons anyway. No,
the exploits of the fellow I am referring to are well known to
youth and adults alike the world over. They have been immor-
talized in songs sung by Louis Armstrong, Tom Jones, Paul
McCartney, Nancy Sinatra, Tina Turner, and Sheryl Crow.

It is Georgi Rosenblum. Well, at least that's what we
think his real name was. He was also known as Sigmund
Rosenblum, also known as Sigmund Reilly, also known as
Sidney Reilly, also known as . . .

You know him as James Bond. Or, more accurately, you know him as the basis for Ian Fleming's fictional character of that name. "Reilly, Sidney Reilly," one imagines him saying as he coolly lights a cigarette and adjusts his bow tie before laying down a royal flush in some smoke-filled casino on the French Riviera. One of the few surviving photographs of Reilly shows him wearing—no kidding—a tuxedo. In 1925, Soviet OGPU agents lured him back into Russia and nabbed him. They thought him a real snappy dresser.

Reilly wore a "demonstratively elegant suit," observed one of his captors.[1]

Jealous of his Savile Row tailor, they shot him. To honor Reilly, the *Evening Standard* ran a series of articles titled "Master Spy," glorifying his career. Fleming picked up the story and ran with it. There is some question about whether he really drove an Aston Martin with rocket-launcher headlamps or flew a space shuttle full of Amazonians, but one thing is certain: "He had a gift for deception," said one biographer.

That's a nice way of saying that he was a clever liar. Reilly had so many aliases, so many different versions of his past and wartime exploits, that John Kerry would be impressed. Even his biographers cannot agree on the broad outlines of his life. To read two Reilly biographies is to read the biographies of two different men.

And that is fitting given his country of origin, because historians cannot agree on the history of Ukraine. There are two different biographies, so to speak—the Western version and the old Soviet version. The bone of contention is something called the *Norman theory* (or *Normanist theory*), which hypothesizes that the first Russian or Ukrainian state was founded neither by Russians nor Ukrainians. Normans founded it. They were also known as Vikings, also known as Varangians, also known as Norsemen . . .

Everyone knew them as nasty brutes with cool names like Hagar and Beowulf. They, too, were snappy dressers, their bodies covered with the hides of wild beasts and their heads crowned with helmets in the style of a Wagnerian opera. (This ensemble was much more attention grabbing than any tuxedo.)

The Norman theory states that government in Ukraine was so chaotic in the ninth century that a delegation was sent north to the Vikings to request their intervention. Like members of any good chamber of commerce, they made their best pitch: "Our land is great and rich, but there is no order in it. Come and rule and reign over us." The Vikings had a bad habit of ruling and reigning over people who had never extended such invitations, so this was an unusual request, to say the least. Still, having laid waste to much of Western Europe, they were bored, and this offered them a new challenge. Chaos was not new to them. Something like literate Mongols who preferred ships to horses, the Vikings created havoc everywhere they went. But creating *order* out of *disorder* was something new, indeed.

Popping a Led Zeppelin CD into the longship stereo,

they sailed south, singing, *"We come from the land of the ice and snow . . ."*[2] Upon arrival, they established what became known as the Rurik Dynasty, after the first king of the new territory, Rurik. Things improved markedly as a result of Viking influence. So much so that Western visitors to Kiev spoke of it as a great and prosperous city. Then the Mongols invaded. Things went downhill from there. Since then, all efforts to move things back to the top of the cultural hill have been Sisyphean in nature.

So what's so controversial about the Norman theory? Russians and Ukrainians have never liked the idea that they needed outsiders—Vikings, of all people—to bring order to their land. When Gerhard Müller, the official historian of Imperial Russia, first presented this theory at a meeting of the Academy of Sciences in St. Petersburg in 1749, he was shouted down. "You dishonor our nation!" he was told. Afterward, Empress Elizabeth ordered his research seized and destroyed. Perhaps Herr Müller would like to do a little research on the history of Siberia? Gerhard got the hint.

And, until quite recently, that is the way history was written in the old Soviet Union. Not according to what actually happened, but according to official policy. Philosopher George Santayana is famously quoted as saying something on the order of, "Those who do not learn from the past are condemned to repeat it." There was another option that George, a naive American, overlooked. *They can rewrite it.* And rewrite it they did. Stalin set the standard, writing some histories himself. Of course, in his own version, he was a hero while many others were completely obliterated from the past.

He even changed the present. When the Red Army overran Hitler's bunker in Berlin in May 1945, Marshal Georgi Zhukov told General Dwight Eisenhower that Hitler was dead. Hitler had, he reported truthfully, committed suicide. Zhukov had seen the body. Still, Stalin, preferring another version of events, sent henchman Andrei Vyshinsky to inform Zhukov of the politically correct view of things. "Hitler is alive," Zhukov now told Eisenhower. Stunned by this reversal, the Western powers launched a massive Osama bin Laden–like search for Hitler. In spite of the fact that the Russians knew, beyond the shadow of a doubt, that Hitler was dead, this would remain the official Soviet "history" until 1968.

After Stalin's death in March 1953, Khrushchev denounced Stalin and these policies at a Party Congress. As Khrushchev spoke, a voice from the back of the room asked why he didn't criticize Stalin when he was alive. Khrushchev stopped suddenly and asked, "Who said that?" There was silence. Again he asked, "Who said that?" Still, no one spoke up. "*Now* you understand," he said.

Whether it is family history or the history of a nation, the narrative of one's past is critical to identity. To be a Kennedy or a Scot or a Native American means something. In this sense, our families give us our identities. They serve as our memory for things we have not seen or cannot remember. Our parents tell us stories from our childhoods. Our grandparents tell us stories about our parents and great-grandparents. In so doing, they teach us something of who our forebears were and who we are supposed to be. We either try to live up to our heritage, or simply try to live it down. Either way, it defines us. But when there are no parents or grandparents to relate the things of the past, a child is robbed of something very precious.

Isn't it interesting that of the thirty-nine books of the Old Testament, twelve are histories? Moreover, the God of Israel commanded that those histories be told repeatedly and commemorated regularly with monuments and feasts. Without annulling family or national character, the Lord sought to give his people an identity that transcended both, creating so lofty a vision of brotherhood that they would be nothing less than children of God, or what Augustine called citizens of the "City of God."

Russia and Ukraine suffer from great identity crises, so thoroughly has the past been rewritten or altogether annihilated. Consequently, society stumbles along in a schizophrenic manner, oscillating between Oriental despotism and earnest efforts to reform and Westernize. In the midst of it all lies a fledgling church, small but not insignificant, working, trusting in the power of God to transform lives and, by extension, culture itself. It is taking root. The goal is neither to Westernize nor to revert to the past, but to Christianize. It offers these countries a new and better identity. It will be interesting to see Eastern Europe in, say, fifty years, and then to compare it to America, where there has been a century-long slow leak of Christianity out of the culture. Perhaps they will be sending missionaries to us.

NOW THAT SASHA WAS OFFICIALLY A MEMBER OF OUR FAMILY, she spent her days passing the time with us in our Odessa apartment. The next step was to obtain her Ukrainian passport. Once that was issued, we would then fly to Kiev, the capital of Ukraine, to obtain permission from the United States government to bring Sasha home.

For Lauri and the boys, these days were mostly boring—doing school, laundry, grocery shopping, preparing meals, and waiting for the call to do the next thing in this adoption process. None of it was boring to Sasha. For her, each day was full of wonder and excitement. She sang and hummed songs constantly and skipped everywhere. At bedtime, she gave hugs all around and nestled into the blankets with the kind of satisfaction one rarely sees. Within minutes, she would be asleep. Her sleep was deep but restless, punctuated by occasional muttering in Russian.

We were learning a lot about Sasha. What impressed me most was her remarkable resilience. She has a great sense of humor. This was a gift from God. Humor can serve as a pontoon in troubled waters, and Sasha has an abundance of it. She liked to play little jokes—hiding around corners, mimicking my (poor and extremely limited) Russian, teasing the boys, and so on. One night I tried to help her put on a new housecoat. Not being familiar with such things, I incorrectly tied it at her waist. (You see, there is a tie on the inside as well as on the outside, and I . . .) She showed Lauri what I had done and laughed uproariously.

Her English was also improving. If you had then met her for the first time, you would not know it. But we could see modest progress. Walking through a park on the Black Sea, we decided to let her ride on a children's train. Unfortunately, the woman selling the tickets spoke not a word of English. Sasha interceded. Again, she could not speak much English, but her experience with us had given her insight into what we did and did not understand, thus making her a fairly effective interpreter. She understood what I wanted to know. She spoke to the woman and turned to me, "For me, ten hryvnia. For"—here she pointed at me—"twenty hryvnia." Translation: *For children, it costs ten hryvnia; for adults, twenty hryvnia.* Off we went on our train ride, Sasha smiling triumphantly the whole way.

MUCH TO VIKTOR'S SURPRISE, WE RECEIVED WORD THAT SASHA'S Ukrainian passport was ready. I immediately booked a flight for Kiev. With our dealings with the Ukrainian government at an end, we said our good-byes to Viktor. A kind and honest man, he had been indispensable to us. Our intrepid facilitator had led us through much more than Ukrainian bureaucracy; he had served as an invaluable intermediary between Sasha and us during these critical early days.

Viktor's advice had been sound, and he always seemed to have our interests in mind. We would miss him.

A couple of hours later, a little twin-prop airplane lifted off from Odessa, carrying us northward. Sasha studied intently the grid-like contours of the city below. In it were contained all of the things of her previous life. The orphanage had denied her a narrative beyond that which she could remember. It was as if she had been born in a vacuum, the first of her kind, having no mother, no father, no heritage, and, statistically, no future.

Not now. Gaining speed and altitude, Odessa faded in a white mist, as did something of Sasha's past and the script that this graceless society had determined her life should follow. With every passing day, Sasha became something different from what she had been. Her transformation had very observable physical manifestations. She carried herself with more self-assurance, like a girl who was, for the first time, regaining her balance after a long and terrible fall. Possessed of an iron will yet buoyed by a ready humor, Sasha wanted to assimilate into our family and start life anew.

Briefly, she turned from the window and took Lauri's hand in both of hers. Finding me across the aisle, she offered a toothy grin and then fixed her eyes on the north ern horizon. She gave the strong impression of a little girl who was looking forward with all her might, having no interest whatsoever in looking back. She was discovering a new identity—not that of an orphan but of someone with an earthly family and citizenship in the heavenly City of God.

SIXTEEN

Out of the Mouth of Babes

*Out of the mouth of babes and infants, you have
established strength because of your foes, to still the
enemy and the avenger.*

—PSALM 8:2

THESE DAYS, MUCH IS MADE OUT OF THE EVIDENCE—OR, AS
some would have it, the *lack* of evidence—for God's existence.
The current focus of this debate is over something called the
"design argument." The Bible itself makes repeated claims
that God's hand, or design, can be seen in creation: "The heav-
ens declare the glory of God, and the sky above proclaims his
handiwork," observed the psalmist (Psalm 19:1). According
to John's gospel, "all things were made through him, and
without him was not any thing made that was made" (1:3).
But it is in Romans 1:18–21 that we find the argument developed most fully. There the apostle Paul writes:

> For the wrath of God is revealed from heaven against all
> ungodliness and unrighteousness of men, who by their

163

unrighteousness suppress the truth. For what can be known about God is plain to them, because God has shown it to them. For his invisible attributes, namely, his eternal power and divine nature, have been clearly perceived, ever since the creation of the world, in the things that have been made. So they are without excuse. For although they knew God, they did not honor him as God or give thanks to him, but they became futile in their thinking, and their foolish hearts were darkened.

In other words, God has not hidden himself from mankind but has, on the contrary, revealed something of his divinity in the cosmos, and while this revelation may not be sufficient to make you a Christian, it is certainly enough to make you a theist. It is a marker—a breadcrumb, so to speak—that, when followed, will lead you to God.

Of course, it is necessary that we look for these markers. When Yuri Gagarin, the Soviet cosmonaut, became the first man to travel into space in April 1961, Khrushchev remarked, "Gagarin flew into space, but didn't see any God there,"[1] to the laughter of the communist world. C. S. Lewis, upon hearing this story, wrote, "Those who do not find Him on earth are unlikely to find Him in space."[2] Lewis's point? A man launched into orbit won't see God's design in the things of heaven if he didn't first see it in the things of earth.

For their part, the atheistic scientific community maintains that there only *appears* to be design in nature. They have constructed sophisticated arguments against design and a Designer—and that is just what you should expect, because it takes a very clever fellow to deny what is obvious to a child. And it is children that I am thinking of here, or more accurately, a child—*Sasha*. As Christians, we made Sasha's spiritual education a priority. How much, we wondered, did she already know and understand? Would we be starting from scratch?

Then again, one never really starts from scratch with children. The design argument is only half of God's natural revelation. There is another marker. The apostle Paul unveiled it in Romans 2:15, telling us that the laws of God are written upon the human heart. That is, we are born with an innate predisposition to believe in the transcendent. Conscience, the soul's voice, serves as the tablet upon which this law is written, and it bears witness not only to our moral responsibilities but also to the existence of God.

Once again, opponents of religion respond with a series of predictable arguments: theism is an accident of birth, wishful thinking, or a "mental 'virus.'" "Part of what I want to say," writes Richard Dawkins, "is that it doesn't matter what particular style of nonsense infects the child brain. Once infected, the child will grow up and infect the next generation with the same nonsense, whatever it happens to be."[3]

There is a great deal of truth to this statement. Indeed, I am thoroughly convinced that Dawkins and his ilk are infecting the brains of many children with their atheistic nonsense, and having done so, there is a very good possibility that this same nonsense will infect the next generation.

As we have already seen, a society contaminated with the virus of unbelief is a pitiless one. The New Atheists, however, aren't keen readers of history. Neither are they astute observers of human nature. Far from being a brain disease, man's religious impulse is natural. So goes the biblical claim, anyway.

But it is more than a biblical claim. According to the recent work of Dr. Olivera Petrovich, a developmental psychologist at the University of Oxford, children are hardwired to believe in God. In a cross-cultural study of British and Japanese children who were shown photographs of man-made and natural objects and then asked to explain how those objects came into existence, children predominantly chose the theological explanation. Reflecting on these results, Dr. Petrovich told me:

> The pattern of responding among Japanese children is highly significant in this context seeing that those children live in a culture that does not in any way encourage a belief in God as creator. Indeed, I was told by my Japanese colleagues that my questions about the origins of objects may not make much sense to Japanese children because it is not part of their experience and culture. Yet, the most common reply given by Japanese preschoolers about natural objects' origins was "Kamisama! God! God made it." Whilst there is growing research evidence that children from across different religious and cultural backgrounds consistently attribute to God the existence of natural objects, what is

so interesting about the Japanese participants is that this particular causal inference is not a product of their education but a natural development in their understanding of the world.[4]

Interesting, yes, but this shouldn't come as a surprise to any of us with children. My Christian readers might reasonably think that their sons' or daughters' belief in Jesus Christ is a result of their own careful instruction. It is. Dr. Petrovich's research, like the biblical claim, suggests that we are innately *religious*. The tenets of a specific faith, however, must be taught. Nevertheless, God has so ordered things that children are ready to receive that instruction. Unbelief, by contrast, is unnatural. One arrives at such a position either because his parents or teachers destroyed his religious sentiment or, if of his own will, because he suppressed much of what his mind and senses told him about the reality of things seen and unseen. "Atheism is definitely an acquired position," says Dr. Petrovich.

Sasha had received little by way of religious education. In some orphanages, Christian teaching was forbidden altogether. One American missionary told me that at the orphanage where she regularly volunteered her time, the director had strictly warned her not to share any of her Christian beliefs with the children. Fortunately, this was not the case at #17. There, the director had permitted Christian missionaries and other volunteers to have some interaction with the children. The instruction, however, was multifarious and sporadic. As a consequence, to Sasha's innate religious bent was added a hodgepodge of Russian Orthodox, Protestant, and decidedly pagan ideas. All of these were interpreted in the light of the prevailing orphanage philosophy.

I am not now referring to atheistic social engineers like Lunacharsky and Makarenko, who had dreamed up the whole awful institution. Rather, I mean the manner in which the children themselves understood the world and their place in it. This philosophy was forged on the anvil of orphanage life and expressed itself in what Arkady had called "jungle law." Part of the law of this jungle was that orphans were unworthy of anything good. Ukrainian society inferred it. Some of their caregivers said it. And the children reinforced it. That this was Sasha's view of things was often manifested in unexpected moments.

"Sasha, I told you not to do that!" Lauri said impatiently. Broken glass lay all over the kitchen floor. Sasha had tried to carry more dishes from the table than Lauri had thought prudent. After a moment, Lauri collected herself.

"Sasha, I am sorry for raising my voice at you. I know you were only trying to help."

"That's okay," Sasha said. "You don't have to apologize to me. I'm different."

Lauri paused from gathering the larger shards of glass and looked up. "What do you mean, you're *different*?" Sasha then explained that people didn't need to apologize to her because she did not deserve it. Lauri was both distressed and moved.

"No, Sasha," she gently corrected. "You're not *different*. If I do something wrong to you, I need to apologize to you. If you do something wrong to me, you need to apologize to me. Understood?"

Sasha nodded, but the lesson was a hard one for her to take in. Shortly thereafter, I was putting her to bed. As she rubbed the buttons of my shirt between her fingers absent-mindedly, she asked through her broken English, "Did you know my mud-dah?" I knew what she meant, but I decided to ignore it for the moment to remind her that circumstances had changed.

"Of course I know her. I'm married to her!" I said light-heartedly. "She's downstairs!"

"No, silly." She gave a sweet laugh and became grave once more. "I mean the one who give me away." She was still fingering the buttons. "People say she bad."

"They only said that to be mean to you, Sasha." I caressed her cheek tenderly.

"She give me away because I *bad*," she added. "That what people say." At once I felt protective of Sasha and infuriated at those who had wounded her with such evil words.

"No, no, Sasha! She must have loved you very much," I said. "Your mother decided to have you. She must have wanted you to have what she couldn't give to you."

"Really?" Her question was hopeful.

"I am certain of it." I smiled reassuringly. "A mother's love is very deep. We are grateful to her." Sasha was pensive. The notion that either she or her biological mother should be people of dignity and worth was new to her. Watching her try to come to terms with these things and seeing something of the anguish it had caused her, led me to speculate how anyone could deny the existence of the soul.

"Sasha, look at me." I took her little face in my hands. She appeared, I thought, angelic. "God wanted you to be with us. He wanted you to be a part of our family."

"You wanted me?" She was very earnest.

"Yes, we wanted you. And for a year we pursued you." She gripped my hands tightly.

"Did God tell you about me?"

"Yes, he did."

If Orphanage #17 did little to hone Sasha's innate religious sentiments and guide them to their proper object of worship, it did not annihilate them either. As moments like this reveal, Sasha was ready to hear the gospel. First, however, we had to cut down the mental forests that served to obscure her understanding of it. Her religious ideas were confused, to say the least: people light candles and cross themselves when they pray; what are crosses? Jesus was not God; Jesus died for sins; God punishes people who are not good; people who are good go to heaven.

This is a fair representation of what she had been able to pick up from her modest interactions with religious people. Filtered through the creed by which these children lived, this grab bag of religious ideas became something altogether different: we should light candles and cross ourselves, as it does something good; we pray to God, not Jesus;

Jesus had to die because orphans are bad; orphans are being punished by God; people who are not orphans go to heaven.

The doctrine to which she had not been introduced was grace. What she had was a form of religion, but without grace that religion cannot be called Christian. No doubt some fine missionaries had mentioned the doctrine in her presence, but either Sasha had not been listening or she did not comprehend it. Regardless, her life in the orphanage and her understanding of life outside of it conspired against such comprehension. She might well have wondered where one finds examples of grace.

I have often thought that before anyone can grasp the doctrine of saving grace, he must first experience grace in its more common form. Such experience tills the soil of the heart and prepares it for the divine. Once, having been hospitalized after a bully thrust her head through a plate glass window, Sasha prayed. I imagine the kind of prayer that God loves most—the innocent, unsophisticated, and sincere prayer of a child. It was easy for me to imagine it. I have seen her pray. Sasha prayed that she would not have to live in the orphanage anymore. She prayed that God would give her parents and a family.

Two things happened after this sweet petition of the Almighty. A woman named Svetlana, apparently a member of a Messianic congregation, entered Sasha's life. She lived alone. From time to time, she was permitted to take Sasha to her home and even to some sort of church. Precisely what Sasha learned from her is unclear, but there can be no doubt that Svetlana's gentle influence made life in the orphanage a bit more bearable. Then, a small team of short-term missionaries from Birmingham, Alabama, arrived at #17. Among this group were my wife, Lauri, and our three boys. Little did any of us know, perhaps Sasha least of all, the remarkable answer her prayer would receive.

SEVENTEEN

"Regarding Sasha . . ."

*I have found that I have no unusual endowments
of intellect, but this day I resolve that I will be an
uncommon Christian.*

—DAVID LIVINGSTONE

EVERY YEAR, THOUSANDS OF AMERICAN CHURCHES SEND OUT short-term missionaries to the four corners of the globe. They improve basic water and electrical infrastructure, provide medical care, build homes and churches, distribute Bibles, teach English, and through these humble acts of service, demonstrate the love of Jesus Christ. Some of these missionaries pay their own way. Others raise their support. The teams are diverse, consisting of high school and college students, young professionals and retirees, stay-at-home mothers and high-powered executives—all of whom have taken time from otherwise busy lives to meet the needs of others.

In June 2008, Lauri and our three boys were part of just such a trip to Odessa, Ukraine, a mission of mercy to Orphanage #17. The men worked to improve facilities, while the women and students busied themselves with the children. As the team constructed picnic tables, they also engaged the children in arts-and-crafts activities, sporting events, and even a talent show. By week's end, friendships had flourished as lives were touched.

No life was more affected than Sasha's. She participated in Lauri's Bible class, excitedly trying to answer all of the questions. She sang and danced during the talent show. Above all, she loved game time. Our oldest son, Michael, who was twenty at the time, led this activity. The orphanage grounds did not lend themselves to anything elaborate. There were no soccer or baseball fields and no gymnasiums or swimming pools. Indeed, there was precious little grass. Even so, with

Photo by Christopher Taunton

Michael with Sasha during a mission trip to Orphanage #17.

the aid of other students on the team, Michael made good use of what was available, playing tag, Frisbee, and similar games with the children. Not surprisingly, they loved it.

More than the games themselves, however, Sasha loved Michael. She became something of a sidekick, following him everywhere. So much so that the team started jokingly referring to her as "Sasha Taunton." At the end of each day, she would say good-bye to him and await his arrival eagerly the next morning. As their time at #17 drew to a close, Lauri and the boys considered what they might do for Sasha. She would, they knew, take the team's departure hard. Not surprisingly, they discussed adoption. Making inquiry of the orphanage director, Lauri discovered that Sasha was available for adoption. She also discovered that Sasha had an incurable disease.

Sasha was HIV-positive. Lauri wept.

BACK IN BIRMINGHAM, ALABAMA, I WAS UNAWARE OF ANY OF this, consumed as I was with work. Lauri and I had discussed adoption many times. Younger than most parents with children the ages of our boys, we had often thought that we would like to provide a home to a child in need, but something always held us back—finances, timing, a lack of consensus between us—something. When Lauri left to go on this mission trip, the thought had occurred to me that she might come back wanting to adopt. I know Lauri, her heart, and more than that, I recollected what happened the last time she went on a trip of this kind—she returned with a heavy heart for the children she had encountered. That started the discussion between us, and while we did not adopt at that time, the Lord moved Lauri to begin circulating photos of those children via e-mail. As a consequence, a child was adopted.

But this was different. Sasha was not the infant we had discussed on previous occasions, and she was a "special needs" child. What to do? Michael e-mailed me the whole story:

> While we've been over here we have connected with an energetic, almost fearless, and all in all a vivacious ten-year-old girl named Sasha. She's practically been my shadow for the past several days, and there's hardly a picture that I'm in that Sasha can't be found somewhere in the background (or, much more likely, front and center, as that seems to be her place of preference!).
>
> She's been shuffled from one orphanage to another since birth, which means that she's considered "adoptable." I actually hadn't thought too much about that, though, until mom told me yesterday morning that she hadn't been able to stop thinking about her (Sasha is in her small group), and mentioned checking to see if she was available for adoption. I encouraged her to check, thinking it was a wonderful idea. So she did.
>
> And that led to our discovery this afternoon—one that was very heart wrenching. We discovered that, though Sasha is adoptable, she is one of four children at #17 who has AIDS. I was absolutely shocked . . . But according to

the orphanage director, she does in fact have AIDS. Mom does kinda wonder about this and thinks that maybe she is HIV-positive and hasn't yet developed AIDS. Still, we both feel rather devastated by this discovery as we sit here and imagine her and her future, where we were earlier imagining her in our future.

So this has not been a lighthearted afternoon, and I think both of us have been thinking a lot about all of this (and have even shed tears over it). You have talked before about knowing why you were in a particular place at a particular time, and I very much have that feeling right now . . . There is so much that this girl needs that we could provide her! A loving home that she has never had! Perhaps medicine . . . But the greatest thing we can provide for her, even greater than our love, would be the hope of the Gospel!

Anyway, I'm sure you're "catching my drift" at this point, and you may just write it off as an emotional response to bad news, which maybe it is, though I don't think I'm given to that. And you can think of all of the negatives of getting ourselves into such a tragic situation, and there would be a lot of them from a worldly perspective . . . As you have often pointed out, Christ tells us that "that which you do to the least of these, you do to me also." Here we have a fantastic opportunity to do so much for someone who has sooo little.

Think about it; my opinion only grows all the stronger as I write . . .

From Ukraine with love, Michael

177

Lauri then followed up this e-mail with one of her own:

My dear,

I was sitting beside Michael as he sent you his e-mail, so I know you have the general picture regarding Sasha. I feel shock and heartache. It is truly quite unbelievable and nothing I ever expected to hear. I am glad you are there to turn to with this difficult issue. I am also equally glad that you are a man with great compassion for people and I can trust you in this.

There are so many difficult things in this. I know you already have thought of many of them. I don't even know if we could bring a child who is diagnosed with HIV into the USA. Please, please give this careful prayer and thought. I want to do what we feel God wants us to do. If He has this difficult thing prepared for us I want Him to use us . . .

I love you!

Lauri

My response was as follows:

Lauri,

Regarding Sasha, I am not against adoption, be it a child with or without HIV. But we don't have that kind of money sitting around, and we have both discussed the very expensive and prolonged process involved in this before. Again, I am not opposed beyond the reasons that you and I have outlined before and quite recently, too. So, until we know what is involved in this, I don't think I can give any kind of meaningful response. I am open. Beyond that, I don't know.

Much love,

Larry

According to statistics, some 35 million people suffer from HIV/AIDS worldwide. "There are lies, damn lies, and then there are statistics," Mark Twain is famously quoted as saying. Statistics, though helpful on certain points, like, say, batting averages and miles per gallon, can deceive on others because it makes flesh-and-blood issues seem rather abstract. The knowledge, for instance, that there were 8 million victims of the Holocaust will never affect you as much as a trip to Auschwitz. Similarly, the 35 million statistic did not hit home with me until Lauri and the boys told me about Sasha. In almost every other respect, she is a little girl like any other, and yet, by no fault of her own, a disease attacks her body.

One should never take adoption lightly under any circumstances, but this was more than we had anticipated. It was a potentially massive commitment. When Lauri came home, we had long walks and talks about Sasha and the possibility of adopting her. There were a lot of unanswered questions. First, there was adoption itself. Not having met Sasha, I felt much more detached from the situation. What about the cost? Could I afford the time involved in such a process? What did the boys think?

"We should adopt her," Michael declared.

"What do you mean 'we'?" I said with a smile. "You won't be here. You'll graduate from college and be gone. A lot of help you'll be!"

Christopher and Zachary were equally emphatic.

"We will help."

"Well, you'd better break open your piggy banks, then, because that's the kind of help I'm going to need." I was pleased to see our boys motivated by Christian conviction.

And then there was the question of Sasha's HIV, and this loomed large in our minds. I confess that I knew virtually nothing about HIV, or its more advanced stage, AIDS. When I thought of it, if I ever thought of it at all, I generally associated the disease with homosexuals or the Third World. Furthermore, my ignorance was such that I didn't know the degree of communicability. Is it possible to get it from a toilet seat or from someone sneezing on you? I didn't know. Our principal concern was whether or not we were putting our children (or other people) at risk.

Fortunately, I knew I was ignorant. Lauri told me so. We sought out specialists in the field of HIV. Lauri, a registered nurse, needed to ask fewer questions than I did, but we still submitted a number of them. In addition, we consulted researchers, the Centers for Disease Control, and individuals and their families who were coping with the disease.

With every question answered to our satisfaction on the medical front, we began to consider issues secondary to the disease. Chief among these were the social ramifications. A child with a cleft palate or spina bifida will bring a much different response from some people than a child who is HIV-positive. The very mention of the virus elicits fear in many. How would we respond if Sasha's name was marked off a party list, or if mothers, ignorant of the disease, pulled their kids out of the pool because Sasha got in it? Discussing the matter with an atheist friend, he remarked, "If you do adopt this little girl, you'll become social pariahs. Yes, we're going to find out just how Christian the people at your church really are." The comment was cynical, and truthfully, I had no idea whether his cynicism was justified or not.

Of course, there was always the option of telling no one about Sasha's condition. One physician advised us to do precisely that. "She's no threat to their health," he said. "Quite the opposite. They are a threat to *her* health."

True, but that was somewhat beside the point. It was how people *perceived* the disease. I knew. After all, I had been, only a short time ago, as ignorant as most of them.

"Okay, then. Let me give you a scenario." I wanted to test the practicality of this approach. "Suppose Sasha is invited to spend the night at a friend's house. Do you think we should tell the parents that she's HIV-positive?" I asked.

"Well, you might *then*," came the response.

"Three men can keep a secret," wrote Benjamin Franklin, "if two of them are dead." The idea that you could reveal such information to only a privileged few was, to my mind, naive. Regardless, Lauri and I felt that it was not our place to make that decision for other people.

"I wouldn't tell anyone," another advised.

"Really? What if she had, say, leukemia? Would you tell me to keep that a secret too?"

"Well, I *guess* not."

Sasha's condition was no embarrassment to her, and I resented the notion that we should act as though it was. She had inherited the disease. No, Lauri and I felt very strongly that trying to keep the matter secret would eventually do more harm than good. It placed a heavy burden on the entire family and implicitly suggested there was something shameful about her illness. Why else do people keep secrets? Still, there was the matter of how some might react. Was it a lose-lose proposition?

One of the advantages of serving as Fixed Point Foundation's executive director is working with so many fine Christian ministers. Where most church members have only one pastor, I have the benefit of several. Discouraged, I sought the counsel of a man who has always been a source of encouragement to me—Frank Limehouse, dean of Cathedral Church of the Advent. Frank is a man of grace and courage. His humility and love for the Lord are evident in his sermons and his actions. Moreover, he had worked in an AIDS ward and possessed knowledge I needed.

Settling into a chair in his office in downtown Birmingham, I felt a heaviness of heart as I considered Sasha's adoption. We had just discussed the subject over lunch. Now, looking out of the window at the leafless trees on a gray fall afternoon, I put my question to him.

"Frank, how do you think people at a typical church would react if our family showed up with an HIV-positive child? Do you think they would act like Christians or be fearful?"

He thought for a moment. "They would probably try to act like Christians and be fearful."

"But—"

"But what?" he interrupted. "*The heck with them!* If this is a door God has opened, you *must* walk through it." Candid to a fault, if ever a man was aptly named, it is Frank. The sentiment was well received. More than that, it was what I needed to hear. I left his office a little taller than I had entered it.

Nevertheless, the biggest hurdle remained: money. Without it, all of this was a moot point. We needed thousands of dollars. Humbling myself, I made a list of some people who might be willing to help.

"Put me down for $10,000, Larry," one said. "Call me if you need any more." I was overwhelmed by this generosity.

"I'll commit $5,000," said another. The next day, he called me back. "I discussed this with the wife last night," he told me. "She wants me to make it $10,000."

Was the Lord opening doors? It seemed as though he were kicking them in. Christian men and women, moved by the grace of God, began stepping forward and paving the way for Sasha's redemption.

Now that adoption seemed like a real possibility, I sat down at a local Starbucks with Dan Edwards, the children's minister at my own church.

"Dan, I think we're going to adopt Sasha."

"Terrific!" he declared unequivocally.

"Well, I appreciate that." I was like a wet blanket on the fire of his enthusiasm. "But you should give careful consideration to the question of whether you want her to participate in Sunday school and that sort of thing."

"What?" He looked puzzled. "So what if she's HIV-positive? Bring her." The matter was settled in his mind.

The paper cup felt especially hot in my hands. "Dan, to you she's a cute little girl who needs a home. But some might not be able to see past the HIV."

He paused thoughtfully before tossing back more of his vanilla-spiked coffee. "Okay, now I see what you mean. What do you suggest?"

Together we made arrangements for an HIV specialist from the University of Alabama–Birmingham to address the church staff. Lauri and I would not attend. The idea was to familiarize them with the disease and to permit them to ask whatever they wanted without any pressure from us. If they then decided that it was best for Sasha not to participate in the children's programs, we would honor their wishes.

"If you're able to adopt her, bring her to church." Bill Hay, Covenant's senior pastor, was as casual as ever after the HIV seminar.

"So you're comfortable with that?" I asked.

"Absolutely," he said off-handedly. "There's never been a

question about that." He paused and then added smilingly, "*This* is what it means to live the gospel."

A few days later, I again saw Frank Limehouse. He pressed a check into my hand. "That's from the people of Advent. You get that little girl and bring her home."

EIGHTEEN

May Day

Give me your tired, your poor,
Your huddled masses yearning to breathe free,
The wretched refuse of your teeming shore.
Send these, the homeless, tempest-tost to me,
I lift my lamp beside the golden door!

—"THE NEW COLOSSUS" BY EMMA LAZARUS,
AS IT APPEARS ON THE STATUE OF LIBERTY

SASHA STARED OUT THE WINDOW FOR THE DURATION OF THE hour-long flight from Odessa to Kiev. As the plane banked for our final approach, she sat up excitedly while Christopher and Zachary stowed their books and iPods. Kiev's broad avenues and onion-domed churches came into view as we dipped below the cloud deck. Ivan, who had seen us off on our journey more than a month before, was waiting.

"Welcome back to Kiev!" he greeted us in his expansive, friendly manner. Sasha, looking a little wary, mumbled something in Russian. Ivan replied to her and then explained.

"She wants to know where Viktor is," he said with a

laugh. "The children always like him." Taking a suitcase, he added, "Don't worry, Sasha. Just a few more steps and you'll be going home with your new family."

The steps Ivan was referring to involved the U.S. government. The United States Citizenship and Immigration Service (USCIS) in Moscow, which had jurisdiction over Ukraine, explained in an e-mail to us what remained to be done:

> Our USCIS Moscow Field Office has authority for adjudicating all inadmissibility waivers in the former Soviet Union. As the child will be inadmissible due to medical reasons (HIV), the adoptive parents will need to file an I-601 waiver in Kyiv [Kiev] . . . the U.S. Embassy in Kyiv will forward the waiver and other supplementary materials to us [upon approval from the CDC], and we will expeditiously adjudicate the waiver. If the waiver is approved, the U.S. Embassy in Kyiv will then issue the adopted child's immigrant visa.

In short, we needed the cooperation of three U.S. agencies if we were to take Sasha home: the U.S. Embassy in Kiev, the Centers for Disease Control in Atlanta, and the USCIS Moscow Field Office. If all went according to plan, Sasha would possess a visa to enter the United States in a matter of days.

Two words in this e-mail filled me with hope: "expeditiously" and "if." Nothing in our dealings with the Ukrainian government had ever been expeditious. As for the *if*, well, it didn't carry the negative connotations I had grown so used to in the old East Bloc. It was that joyously optimistic American *if.*

When Lauri, Sasha, and I arrived at the embassy, the place appeared to be under siege. A mass of people stood all along the heavy fencing, both inside and outside of the compound. It reminded me of scenes from Saigon in 1975 or Tehran in 1979. But these were not angry people. They were Ukrainians seeking visas to America. Judging from the line, I thought we might be waiting for days.

"This way, sir," an armed officer said, directing me to a typical government-issue building that stood just beyond the security checkpoint. As I looked back at the queue that wound snakelike over the embassy grounds, he noted my confusion. "You're citizens of the United States. You don't wait in *that* line."

Passing through another security point and into a small anteroom, we took a number and waited to be summoned. Aside from a few Americans who seemed to be adoptive parents like us, the room was full of Ukrainians. The air virtually throbbed with their hopes and dreams. I could only guess at how long it had taken them to reach this place, this moment. As names were called, people proceeded to a thick, glass window. Some left it weeping joyously, while others, dejected, departed in silence.

"Taunton?" a woman called over the little speaker. It was our turn.

"How are you, today?" she asked.

"Glad to be here," Lauri replied truthfully.

"Very good." The woman behind the glass greeted Sasha in Russian before getting down to business.

"Here's where we are. We have sent the medical records to the CDC in Atlanta," she told us. "Once we get that back from them, we can then file the I-601 waiver with Moscow. If they approve it, we will then be able to issue her visa."

"How long before that is done?" I asked.

"Typically, about a week from beginning to end." She was preparing me for something. "But we are up against May Day, a Russian and Ukrainian holiday, and that will affect turnaround time."

"I don't understand."

"The United States government observes national holidays in host countries," she explained. "We need to get this visa approved in the next few days, or you could be here for another ten days or so."

"Oh, I see. Can you do anything?"

"We're going to try!" She smiled. "Let's see if we can get the people in Atlanta to move things along for us."

They did. A couple of days later, the CDC notified us that their part was complete. All that remained was the USCIS in Moscow. Shortly thereafter, they, too, had discharged their administrative responsibilities.

"We approved the I-601 waiver and forwarded a scanned copy to the U.S. Embassy in Kyiv," e-mailed an anonymous Moscow officer. "Congratulations and good luck!"

The last line of this e-mail is noteworthy. With the

exception of the SDA officer in Kiev who offered a gracious "Bless you" to us as we departed her office, these simple expressions of kindness had been absent in our dealings with every Ukrainian government official we had encountered. Malevolence had been the order of the day. With the CDC, the U.S. Embassy, and the USCIS Moscow Field Office, however, there was no spitting or whipping. There were no bribes, no abrupt appointment cancellations, and no petty expressions of power. Sasha was a child they wanted to help, and keeping her in the country for another week while documents were signed, copied, and filed seemed unreasonable to them. The contrast was striking and representative of two entirely different cultures.

Paperwork completed, the U.S. Embassy issued her visa.

"You're going to America, Sasha," the embassy worker told her. Sasha grinned, not fully understanding, but knowing that it must be good.

The next day was Friday, May 1st—May Day. Also known as International Workers' Day, it remains a major socialist holiday in Eastern Europe. As we piled our luggage into a van for the drive to the airport, thousands of old communists, nostalgic for the ironfisted regime of Joseph Stalin, marched down Khreshchatyk street with red banners and hammer-and-sickle flags. So what if millions of people had disappeared under Soviet rule? Those were, the marchers seemed to be saying, the good old days.

Like so much else in that part of the world, socialists hijacked the holiday. May Day was once a celebration of spring and rebirth. For that reason, it was an appropriate occasion for Sasha's exodus. She was, in a sense, being reborn.

Our route home required a one-night layover in Paris. There are, I assure you, worse places to spend an evening. Standing in line to have our passports inspected by a French border officer at Charles De Gaulle Airport, we discovered a problem. Sasha, not yet a U.S. citizen and traveling on a Ukrainian passport, could not enter France without a visa. The rest of us were fine, but the law required her to remain in the terminal. Of course, that meant we would all stay in the terminal with her.

"We have adopted her," I explained to the officer. "Can't you make an exception?" He looked at me expressionlessly and then down at Sasha.

"Technically, no," he said. "But it does seem a bit unreasonable. Let me see what I can do." A few minutes later he returned.

"We have issued a twenty-four-hour visa." He then turned to Sasha and smiled. "Enjoy Paris."

And we did. Lauri and I agree that this was one of the more magical nights of our lives. It was late, and everyone was tired. But this was Paris, and neither Lauri nor the kids had ever been there. Sasha had never been outside of Odessa. Taking what bit of money I could spare, I rented a minivan taxi. On a gorgeous spring evening, the city bathed in light, we made our way to most of the major attractions: down the Champs-Élysées, around the Arc de Triomphe, a photo at Notre Dame, past the Louvre, and a sprint to the base of the Eiffel Tower. It wasn't much of a tour, because some things were closed and we did it all in less than two hours, but that was irrelevant. There was a feeling of liberation. And as much as we enjoyed Paris, it was Sasha whom we enjoyed most. It was as if she had entered an enchanted world. The brilliance of the city, the hordes of excited tourists, the extraordinary sights—it all captivated her.

Returning to the airport hotel, Sasha asked, *"Doma?" Home?* It had never occurred to us that she might think this was our house.

Lauri laughed. "No, Sasha. We don't live here!" Having little point of reference, how was she to know otherwise?

"We have one more flight," I tried to explain.

ONE DAY AND ROUGHLY 4,300 MILES LATER, THE DELIVERY WAS complete:

"Ladies and gentlemen, we are making our final approach into Atlanta International Airport. In preparation for landing, please put all seats in their upright position and tray tables up and locked. Any items that need to be stowed..."

According to U.S. adoption laws, the moment the wheels of our Boeing 767 touched down on American soil, Alexandra Lauren Taunton, "Sasha," would become a citizen of the United States of America. There was something powerfully symbolic in that. Her new life would begin in concert with her new citizenship.

"Are we there?" Sasha asked, her voice brimming with excitement.

"Almost," I said, my finger and thumb spaced slightly to indicate *just a little bit more*. Lauri patted her arm reassuringly.

Sasha sat forward, gripping the armrests, her slight frame barely taking up half of the seat. I can only describe her face as one of total exhilaration.

Minutes later, a USCIS officer was inspecting our passports and adoption paperwork. Sasha studied his face with interest. She had never seen a black man before. Amused, he smiled at her and continued his procedure, contacting the CDC and conferring with the officer-on-duty. Satisfied that all was in order, he rose and extended his hand to me.

"Congratulations," he said with a grin. "She is free to enter the country."

"Thank you." I was starting to feel exhilarated too.

"Did you know that she is now a citizen of the United States?" he asked. I imagined that he never tired of this part of his job. I wouldn't have.

"Yes, I did."

Looking down at Sasha, he smiled and turned back to me. "Does she know it?" I briefly surveyed her glowing countenance.

"I think she does."

A week ago, Sasha had never been outside of the orphanage system in Odessa, Ukraine. Now she was literally doing cartwheels at Hartsfield's baggage claim. After almost a year of countless meetings, signatures, inspections, corrupt officials, waiting rooms, spiritual warfare, overseas travel, and emotional highs and lows, it was finished.

The two-hour drive home to Birmingham felt like a victory lap at Talladega. Appropriately, Sasha sang her theme song at regular intervals the whole way—"A-B-C-D-E-F-G . . ."

As we rounded a corner in our neighborhood, our house came into view. Dominating the lawn was a huge banner reading, "WELCOME HOME!" A sweet committee from our church and community had decorated the yard with colorful balloons and streamers, giving the whole house a festive appearance.

Once we were parked in the driveway, Sasha spilled forth from our car and sprinted into Michael's waiting arms. Inside, a veritable banquet awaited us. Our home showed every sign of loving, feminine hands having gone before us to carefully prepare a warm welcome. Indeed, only minutes before, the house had, we were told, been full of women doing precisely that.

"Doma?" Sasha asked. Now that we were in Alabama, she just wanted some reassurance that this wasn't another stop on the way.

"Yes. This is home," I said.

Sasha tried to take it all in—her bedroom; our German shepherd, Blitz; the trampoline; the ice dispenser—all of it. Later that night, Lauri did the work of getting her ready for bed and left me the fun part of tucking her in for the night.

I always—well, usually, anyway—savored this bit with my boys when they, too, were little. I pulled the blankets up under her chin and gave her a gentle squeeze. She sighed contentedly and cuddled her little bear (or pig, or whatever it is) before rolling over to sleep. For a moment, I just gazed at her. Sasha's dark-blonde hair splashed around the pillow, and her face was joyful. In that moment, I knew that I loved her. I hadn't expected that so soon.

Sleeping in the room adjacent to her were two of Sasha's greatest champions. Her brothers, Christopher and Zachary, had consistently exhibited the love of Christ to her. That our son Michael was in favor of adopting Sasha, you already know. But Christopher and Zachary had to do the heavy lifting. Once they expressed their desire to see our family adopt Sasha, they never wavered from it. They endured being away from home and all of the discomforts that entailed without complaint. They bore with patience many trials without contributing to them. And they made Sasha a part of our family. I was proud of them.

Watching her sleep, I was mindful of the struggles that had brought her to this very moment. It all seemed a bit unreal. Like Pam awakening to find Bobby Ewing in the shower and the past year a bad dream on *Dallas*, I felt as though Sasha had always been a member of our family, so well did she fit the scene. And yet, the struggles did happen. Moreover, until then, Sasha had never known family life of any kind, the warmth of a home, a bedroom of her own, clean clothes and a shower every day—none of it. Quietly,

Lauri walked up beside me, leaning a smiling head on my shoulder. Our hearts were soaring.

The next day, the boys and I went to church while Lauri stayed at home with Sasha. The journey had exhausted them both, and the rest was richly deserved. The lesson that morning touched on a subject of interest to many Christians, if the sales of *The Purpose Driven Life* are any indicator—discerning God's will for your life. Over the years, I have met so many people who are distressed by this, as if God's will were some great, nebulous thing to which they do not have access. Rather than a formula, however, I have always thought the matter one of faithfulness in any given moment of our lives.

When our family decided to submit to the Lord's leading in this adoption, I must confess that I had many misgivings. If ever Lauri had them, she did not voice them. But I could think of a hundred variables in this process that could go wrong. Still, God was clearly giving us an option: we could be faithful and experience the great blessing that was in store for us, or we could walk away and forget about the whole thing.

The Lord led us to Sasha. I have told that part of the story. But there is more. Something happened at the court hearing in Odessa that I have not yet related. At a decisive moment in the hearing, the judge asked Sasha if she wanted to be adopted by our family.

"*Da*"—yes—she replied.

"You know that you will be leaving Ukraine, don't you?"

the judge continued. "Wouldn't you rather stay in Ukraine with people who speak Russian?"

"She chose the Tauntons," the orphanage director said, interrupting the interrogation.

"*Stoi*?"—What?—asked the judge.

"She wants to be adopted by *them*," the director explained, indicating our general direction.

"Is this true?" the judge asked Sasha.

"*Da*," Sasha replied, with a shy smile.

You see, while God was at work in our hearts, he was also at work in Sasha's heart. Were it not for her great courage and the steadying hand of Providence, she, too, might have walked away. The pressure to do so came from all sides, not the least being from the judge herself. But Sasha didn't retreat. The Lord sent her flare high into a night sky, and one by one he knocked down any excuses we might have not to rescue the one who had fired it.

Jeremiah 33:3 reads, "Call to me and I will answer you, and will tell you great and hidden things that you have not known." God had directed us to Sasha so that we might be a blessing to her life. The great and hidden thing that we had not known, however, was the tender blessing she would be to our lives.

NINETEEN

Sasha's New Beginning

But Jesus called them to him, saying, "Let the
children come to me, and do not hinder them, for to
such belongs the kingdom of God."

—LUKE 18:16

THE LOST BOYS OF SUDAN, AN EXCELLENT 2008 DOCUMENTARY, chronicles the story of two African refugees' flight from their civil war–torn home and their subsequent journey to America. Orphaned by the war, the boys survive dangers of every kind before escaping their native land—they are pursued by lions, attacked by militia, and forced to endure the hardships of a refugee camp. Finally, their ordeal apparently over, they arrive in the United States. As an American viewer, you are sure that this is the happy ending you have been waiting for. After all, they are safe, right?

On the contrary, their new home holds fresh and subtler dangers—churches offer them sincere but fleeting assistance; the boys frequently hold hands, as friends do in their own culture, only to discover, to their horror, that some think them homosexuals; they are discriminated against by both white *and* black; and the temptations of materialism soon crowd in upon them. As you follow these boys on their journey, you see things through their eyes. As a consequence, you understand something of the troubles of modern Africa. What is particularly insightful, however, is the perspective it offers on American culture too.

So it was with Sasha.

With the Ukrainian part of the adoption behind us, Sasha had begun her new life in America. She had been on this side of the Atlantic for a week, and what a week it had been. Sasha adjusted well to her new environment, and it was all new to her. Throughout, Sasha provided us with something of a lens through which to view our own culture. Sometimes the perspective she provided was amusing; at others, it was sobering.

If you have ever seen the 1964 musical *My Fair Lady*, you will recollect that the plot involves two old bachelors and a bet that one of them can transform a flower girl named Eliza Doolittle into a woman with the bearing of a duchess. After weeks of preparation, the two test her readiness by taking her to a horse race. Initially, all goes well. But then Eliza forgets herself as her horse, Dover, comes down the stretch:

"C'mon, Dovah! Move your bloomin' arse!"

Eyebrows are raised in dignified shock. Eliza's outburst, violating the unwritten and unspoken rules of etiquette, scandalizes the well-to-do. Eliza, the bachelors discover, is not quite ready for a trip beyond the safe and predictable confines of Professor Higgins's London flat.

In these early days, Sasha had a bit of Eliza Doolittle about her. If you travel abroad, you may encounter a new language and a new culture. But you understand the basics of civilization—how a family functions, how to order at a restaurant or buy something at a store, how to behave in public, what to do when someone prays, and so on. For Sasha, however, most of these were new and fascinating things to be discovered and explored. As a consequence, well, the results were occasionally . . .

"C'mon, Dovah! Move your bloomin' . . ."

One night our family attended a Birmingham Barons baseball game. It was our first attempt at taking Sasha out in public. We enjoy these relatively inexpensive outings. On a nice evening, a Coke, hot dog, and a little bat spin relay are hard to beat. Sasha, we had discovered, was, like Eliza, an intensely competitive girl with an interest in sports. Meeting the Baron's mascot, cheering for the home team and *against* their opposition, dancing during the seventh-inning stretch—she liked them all. Did she understand baseball? Not in the slightest. And while her English was improving, she still had some work to do.

As the ubiquitous stadium chant, "We will, we will *rock you*!" cranked up, Sasha decided to join in—only her version was a bit different. It sounded like "Window, window—*vacuum*!" with a heavy Russian accent. For some reason, I tried to correct her English. The improvement was modest at best.

"Vee vill, vee vill—*vacuum!*"

"That version is just fine," Lauri said, reclining comfortably in her seat. "I like that one."

Sasha, unaware that she was pledging herself enthusiastically to a life of servitude, stood with fists pumping the

Photo by Christopher Taunton

Sasha meets the Birmingham Barons' mascot.

air in the full conviction that she was spot-on. I tried to save her, but, alas, to no avail. People stared, but anonymous as we were, we didn't much care. That is, until she caught the eyes of cameramen who projected her image up on the stadium JumboTron.

"Vee vill, vee vill—*vacuum*!" Our boys, used to her by now, watched the game in silence.

The interesting thing one realizes with an Eliza Doolittle in his house is just how many unwritten and unspoken rules there are. Indeed, they are so subtle and so ingrained in me that I am, at this moment, at a loss to think of one. Regardless, Sasha violated a lot of them. I am talking about the many rules that are culture-specific—many of them *American South*–specific. Initially, we grimaced when she would run over one as a Hummer might a Smart Car, but then we just stopped worrying about it. The violation was, after all, purely innocent, and sometimes the social faux pas gave me reason to reflect on why we had that particular rule in the first place.

As for the sobering, upon arrival in the United States, we immediately scheduled Sasha for a battery of doctors' appointments. The first was to the HIV clinic. It lasted three hours. They drew ten vials of blood from her skinny frame. Not even a whimper. Next came the pediatrician. Examining Sasha's teeth, the doctor gasped.

"No American child could endure this so stoically," she told Lauri. Denied proper dental care in the orphanage, a couple of her teeth were black and rotten, the nerves exposed. We were shocked. Since her front teeth looked good, we had assumed the back ones were fine too.

The next day, Lauri told Sasha that I would be taking her to see a dentist. Her eyes widened in horror. When I came home, she was crying. Entering the dentist's office, she was compliant but sat quietly in the waiting room, tears streaming down her cheeks. Dr. Robert Sanderson, himself a Christian who had adopted a child from Guatemala, came out and took a seat next to her.

"Hi there, Sasha," he said gently. "It will be okay. I promise."

She was inconsolable, repeatedly making the downward spiral motion of a drill with her finger. Whatever she had suffered, it had left a lasting and terrible impression upon her.

"They have often been treated without anesthesia," he explained.

As Dr. Sanderson escorted us into the examination room, Sasha began to tremble. Ericka, the dental assistant, had no more success than the rest of us in convincing her that it would be okay. I got an idea.

"Ericka, what if you put me in the chair first and demonstrate on me what you're going to do to her?" Ericka graciously agreed to my little scheme, and since a simple examination and X-rays were the only things on the agenda, it would be easy enough to do.

At first, Sasha watched skeptically, but as Ericka pleasantly poked around my mouth, Sasha began to relax and even to laugh. We exchanged seats, the rest of the appointment went smoothly, and a deeper trust was forged.

When Dr. Sanderson saw her back teeth, though, he, too, gasped. "I'm told that no American child would endure that," I said. He shook his head. "No American *adult* would endure it."

An oral surgeon agreed. "Yikes. This will require a series of surgeries. I recommend that we just knock her out and do it all at once. Less traumatic that way." A few hours and several teeth later, it was all over.

Feeling that she deserved some kind of reward for her ordeal, we bought Sasha a bicycle. Although ten, she had never been taught how to ride a bike. Putting it in the back of my Tahoe, we drove to a nearby exercise trail and started our lessons. The entire time, we practiced on the same stretch of a quarter-mile loop. Placing a hand on her waist or shoulder, I would run beside her while she got the feel of steering, pedaling, and balancing. Repeatedly, she wrecked. Usually, I was able to catch her; occasionally, I was not, and she would hit the ground or the hard asphalt with a thud. Every time, she got right back up, tongue clenched between her lips, more determined than ever to conquer.

As we worked, the same people passed us repeatedly. I knew none of them, but I sensed that they knew this little girl was an underdog. Perhaps it was Sasha's size that gave her away. Most learn to ride a bike at a much younger age. Perhaps it was the fact that she spoke to me in Russian, signaling observers that she was probably adopted. Or maybe it was just the sheer determination with which she assaulted the task. Whatever it was, they encouraged her. And when, after an hour, she took off, no longer in need of my assistance, a general "whoop" went up from the whole park. With a broad smile gracing her face, Sasha propelled the bike forward and took in the encouraging cheers with the enthusiasm of a Tour de France winner.

Photo by Christopher Taunton

Sasha learns how to ride a bike.

Driving home, I was full of admiration for her. *The girl's got moxie*, I thought. Lauri and I had both noticed it. It is a characteristic that would serve Sasha well, for there were untold challenges ahead. Reliving the moment with her family, she referred to herself in the third person. "Sasha"—at this point, she simulated riding a bike. "Papa"—here she mimed running, added panting for special effects, and pointed at me—"like a dog!" Her sense of humor was in full bloom.

TWENTY

Is America Safe?

This is an age of the world when nations are trembling and convulsed. A mighty influence is abroad, surging and heaving the world, as with an earthquake. And is America safe? Every nation that carries in its bosom great and unredressed injustice has in it the elements of this last convulsion.

—FROM HARRIET BEECHER STOWE'S
UNCLE TOM'S CABIN[1]

I HAVE WRITTEN SOME VERY TOUGH THINGS ABOUT UKRAINE and the adoption process in that country. I have given an unvarnished picture of an industry that deals in the exploitation of children and a country that cares little for the "least of these." There is much more that I could say—requests for money (always cash) to destinations unknown, hints of abuse, and rumors of corruption so vile that I will not here repeat them.

No doubt, some readers will be uncomfortable with these characterizations. To buttress their authority on the subject, they will cite a mission trip, a tour, or perhaps some business they have done in that part of the world. To such objections, I can only say that I, too, had been in Ukraine and Eastern Europe many times before adoption took us there. I had led multiple tour groups to Russia, Poland, and the Czech Republic; my work had taken me to Hungary and Ukraine several times; and I had served on short-term mission teams to Russia and Ukraine. On each of these occasions, I enjoyed the experience immensely. Indeed, I am certain that had our family been traveling to Ukraine to serve as missionaries, we would be getting along happily enough. When it comes to international travel, we are a pretty savvy lot.

This was different.

Rather than traveling with other Americans or associating with the host country's Christian population, we were dealing with the government. Even then, had we been simply trying to conduct a business transaction of some kind, the corruption would have been more of a nuisance than fundamentally disturbing. But then, it was a business transaction. We were bargaining with the government for the life of a child. As a consequence, we experienced dramatic emotional highs and lows. One moment, the race would seem near its end, and then we would discover that the finish line had been moved. Always, in the back of our minds, there was this nagging feeling that they might find some reason, however invalid it might be, to deny Sasha the hope of adoption.

And that's precisely what they want to do—stop international adoptions. Why? As Ukraine endeavors to become a full member of the European Union, the government is increasingly sensitive to those things that reflect poorly upon the nation's honor and economic state of affairs. Orphans and orphanages sully both. Currently, there are scarcely credible reports circulating in Ukraine that some 10 percent of all internationally adopted children are either killed for their organs or made sex slaves. The precise origin of this statistic is unclear, but there is no doubt that the government is using it as a pretext for ending these adoptions. Complicating matters is the fact that many believe this dubious report.

"I hear that 10 percent of all children adopted by foreigners have their organs harvested," a Ukrainian businessman said to me upon learning my reason for being in Odessa. He gave a shrug. "I guess it must work out okay for the other 90 percent," he concluded with total seriousness.

Again, while the statistic is almost certainly a gross exaggeration of some horrible anomaly or an urban legend, he believed it. And a 10 percent casualty rate was, in his view, acceptable. As I say, it is a different view of human life.

Of course, not every adoption experience is the same. There are many variables: when the adoption occurred (it is much harder now than in years past), whether the orphanage is private or state-operated, the region of the country, the officials involved, etc. Even so, variables notwithstanding, there are certain constants, too, and chief among them are corruption and the neglect of children.

Some American couples think that they did not pay any bribes. They are naive. "We do not tell Americans what is going on because they do not want to know," one Ukrainian facilitator told me. "Any adoption from Russia or Ukraine will involve plenty of [bribes]. We just estimate them and build them into the overall fee."

Others will tell you that things are not as bad as I have characterized them. People said similar things about slavery: "They are treated like members of the family." Author Malcolm Muggeridge, reflecting on our capacity for self-delusion, wrote, "People, after all, believe lies, not because they are plausibly presented, but because they want to believe them." Muggeridge, who did a bit of traveling in Russia and Ukraine himself, knew what he was talking about.

It is worth noting that it is quite possible to adopt and avoid the ugliness of it all. If one has sufficient means, one can stay in some fashionable hotel, leave the rest to the facilitators, and never set foot in an orphanage until it is time to whisk the child away. Even then, all you have to see is the office. It is when you start to poke around and ask questions that you begin to see just how rotten the whole system really is.

"I was wondering," I began, "was [a certain government official] honest, or was she corrupt like everyone else?"

Ivan gave a cynical smile. "Honest? Please explain this concept! We are unfamiliar with it in Ukraine!" He then gave me the sort of look one might give a child just before telling him that there is no Santa Claus.

"Larry, they are all corrupt. *All of them*. It is simply a question of degrees."

Adoption facilitators will openly acknowledge that the government, at best, tolerates them. "They accuse us of selling children," said another. Such an accusation is rich with irony as these government representatives extort money from adoptive parents. I don't know what we would have done without our facilitators to advise, translate, and help us navigate the minefield that is adoption. Do they profit from it? Sure. The same way, I suppose, a physician profits from the sick. Nevertheless, both provide a valuable service that is worthy of compensation. No, it is the bureaucrats who are selling children. They hold them hostage until the ransom is paid.

It is true that it is not an organized industry or human trafficking as it is commonly understood. There was no central body with whom we dealt whose goal was the exploitation of children. The crime was admittedly *disorganized*. Does that make it any better? Whether it is bribing officials individually or bribing them collectively, the effect is the same—children are being neglected and exploited. In retrospect, I would have preferred crime of the organized type. Then, at least, the process might have been efficient.

Furthermore, I doubt that a single official we encountered fosters an active malice toward orphans. Upon meeting Sasha, some of these same officials were cordial to her, patting her on the head, or even hugging her. Were they sincere? Probably. But that is beside the point. I do no less for my dog—more, in fact. Still, offer me ten thousand dollars and you can have him. I'll even throw in his dish and a doggie bone. What we encountered was a criminal, passive indifference where children were treated like any other commodity, and if you wanted a child, you would have to pay.

Photo by Hannah Slamen

Sasha and her dad, the author.

And there you have it, two competing policies on adoption, both bad, within the same government. At the national level, the government, trying to make Ukraine look as attractive as possible to the EU, wants to hide the plight of their vast orphan population rather than solve it; at the municipal and regional level, a corrupt bureaucracy seeks to parlay foreign interest in Ukrainian orphans into a profitable industry. Conveniently, the propaganda about international adoptions is used (generated?) to the advantage of both—by one to deny adoptions, by the other as leverage for more money from those who want to adopt.

This brings me to my point, a question, really: How does a given society arrive at a place where it not only tolerates such a system but also incubates and nourishes it, callously neglecting its elderly, sick, and orphaned?

WHEN OUR FAMILY FIRST LEFT ALABAMA FOR UKRAINE, MY LATE-night conversation with Christopher Hitchens, only days before, lingered in my mind. Christianity's contributions to society seemed too remote for him and other non-Christians to appreciate what it gave to them on a daily basis. After all, if one enjoys a life of relative peace and prosperity with little input from Christians, one is likely to extrapolate from his or her personal experience to society as a whole. Christianity, one then concludes, is superfluous. This line of reasoning grossly underestimates the degree to which Christianity has informed the moral and intellectual sensibilities of the people and institutions around him. That this was true, I had no doubt. But the argument had an abstract quality that blunted the force of it. *Where does one find common grace?* I had wondered.

At the time I thought the Ukraine trip had nothing whatsoever to do with this question or even with my work as a Christian apologist. Our decision to adopt Sasha was, to be sure, an act motivated by Christian conviction, but one that fit more neatly into some other category of Christian endeavor.

I could not have been more wrong. Psalm 8:2 reads, "Out of the mouth of babes and infants, you have established strength because of your foes, to still the enemy and the avenger." Oh, how true! In a precious little girl, I discovered an argument stronger than any that I, or a hundred apologists of greater intellect, might have devised. *Sasha was the argument.*

In my search for meaningful examples of common grace, the Lord opened my eyes to a world where it was all but absent. Here was a life not gentled by Christian influence, but a life made immeasurably harsher without it. That grace was largely missing from her world was not, as we have seen, an accident of history. It is not to be attributed to Ukrainian national character, a disregard for the poor, bad economic and political policies, corrupt bureaucracies, or even seventy-five years of communist rule. All of these were the result, not the source, of the problem. This country, and others like it, can trace their miseries to either an indifference to Christianity or a willful and systematic suppression of it. In the case of Ukraine, it was the latter, leading to an unwitting cultural suicide. Sasha's whole life and world had been shaped by the kind of aggressive secularism that presently enamors so many in the West. She was a victim of politicians and social engineers of whom the New Atheists could be proud—people who sought (and succeeded) to create a society free from religious influence. The effect was the material, intellectual, and spiritual deprivation of generations of Eastern European children and adults. And while the inventors of the system were long gone, their influence lingered.

Fascists think society's problems are a question of race.

Eliminate the "lower orders" of our species, and you solve everything. Communists think it a question of economics, a class war. Seize private property and redistribute it equally and—*voilá!*—utopia. Atheists think the problem is religion. Environmentalists blame industrialization. Democrats blame Republicans. Republicans blame Democrats. Everyone agrees that there is a problem, but efforts to identify the source of it are incomplete, misguided, or evil.

Lord of the Flies author William Golding was correct in deducing that the defects of human society are the defects of human nature. The prophet Jeremiah said something very similar two and a half millennia earlier: "The heart is deceitful above all things, and desperately sick; who can understand it?" (Jeremiah 17:9). Returning to the question I put to Christopher Hitchens in the restaurant—which religions or philosophies restrain our darker impulses, and which ones exacerbate them?—the best answers are Christianity and atheism, respectively.

As Jesus was being crucified, he said, "Father, forgive them, for they know not what they do" (Luke 23:34). One might argue that this was the case with many of those whose theories led to the atrocities of the twentieth century. Beyond the French Revolution (which should have been sufficient), they had little historical precedent to demonstrate what their misguided notions would lead to. The same, however, cannot be said of the modern atheist syndicate that would give us the twentieth century in perpetual rerun. That Dawkins and his coterie should conclude that

215

the secular horrors of the modern era had nothing whatsoever to do with secularism is more than a lapse in judgment;
it is mendacity of the first order.

Proponents of a society free from religious influence
can point to no nation or civilization that was founded upon
atheistic principles that we might call even remotely good.
The story of those regimes is well documented and may be
summarized in a word—*murderous*. What those proponents
can point to are secular societies that are still running off of
their accumulated Christian capital. But beware. When the
fumes in that tank are spent, tyranny cannot be far away.
How many dictatorships, genocides, purges, wars, famines,
gulags, economic disasters, morally bankrupt leaders, and
impoverished nations must the world suffer before its people
realize that belief in God is necessary for the stability of civilization? George Washington's words were prophetic: "Reason
and experience both forbid us to expect that national morality can prevail in exclusion of religious principle." This he
deduced without the benefit of seeing the twentieth century.
The eighteenth, it seems, was enough.

As a boy in elementary school, I was mischievous.
My pranks, though harmless enough and amusing to my
classmates, were undoubtedly a source of frustration to my
teachers. I was sent to the principal for discipline so frequently that he affectionately referred to me as his "office
aide." I knew the boundaries, where I could push and where
I should not. Punishments were predictable, and even then
I knew I could rely on the mercy of those administering

the discipline. That they adhered to certain rules made my minor life of crime a possibility. I could presume upon their good graces.

So, it seems to me, are the New Atheists. They rail against the Christian God in the full knowledge that his followers are bound by principles—principles upon which these bloodletters presume. "Only a Christian culture could produce a Voltaire or a Nietzsche," T. S. Eliot observed. Indeed, only a Christian culture could produce a Richard Dawkins or a Peter Singer. How long would they last in, say, Iran, were they to denounce Allah? Or in atheistic North Korea or China were they to speak against the government? Not long, I assure you. In this sense, they acknowledge Christianity's beneficence if only unwittingly.

Then again, with the specter of a Muslim Europe looking more possible with every passing year, perhaps they are beginning to recognize that the freedoms they enjoy are due to more than serendipity. In an April 2010 interview with the *Times* of London, Dawkins said, "There are no Christians, as far as I know, blowing up buildings. I am not aware of any Christian suicide bombers. I am not aware of any major Christian denomination that believes the penalty for apostasy is death. I have mixed feelings about the decline of Christianity, in so far as Christianity might be a bulwark against something worse."[2]

This conversion comes better late than never, I suppose. Dare we hope that this is the beginning of a general abandonment of atheism? Probably not. It may, however, indicate that things are getting a bit dicey in North Oxford, and that the elites are nervous.

On the west side of the campus of my undergraduate alma mater, Samford University, there is a building called the Rotunda. It is an attractive edifice, constructed as it is in the Georgian style like the rest of the university. Entering from the north side, visitors are treated to the work of D. Jeffrey Mims, an artist of sublime skill. Gracing the walls are four of his oil paintings depicting miracles from the Bible: Moses bringing forth water from a rock to quench the Israelites' thirst; Jesus giving sight to a blind man; Peter and John mending the broken form of a lame beggar; and Jesus raising the dead son of the widow at Nain. Of these, the fourth struck me most powerfully when first I saw it as a student. The man is withered, his body cold and colorless. Except for his arm. It is there that Jesus is touching him. Radiating outward from the Master's grip, the flesh is warm and pink. So skillfully has the artist rendered this scene that it's easy to imagine that his whole body will soon be likewise restored.

Since the fall of man, there has never been a Christian nation. What there have been are nations with varying degrees of Christian influence. In the parts of those societies touched by Christ, the blood courses, fortifying, revitalizing, and sweeping away contaminants as it goes. At the cold and colorless extremities are those places where the healing power of his Church has not yet penetrated. Here one finds cruelty, injustice, and indifference.

As militant secularists rush to banish Christianity from American public life, I have sought to give you a snapshot of what this country—indeed, what *any* country—will look like should they succeed. For grasping the other arm of America is the hand of unbelief. Its effect is exactly the opposite of Christ's. What it touches, it destroys. That it has already done so to a large degree is evidenced in: the blight of abortion; a

Photo by Christopher Taunton

Sasha and her mom, Lauri.

creeping socialism that many mistake for Christian charity; the breakdown of the family; the advancement of the homosexual agenda; a rapid rise in crime; a corresponding decline in education; and suicides on a scale hitherto unknown. American society itself stands to be orphaned, cut off from its rich Christian heritage. Mercifully, Jesus Christ has not yet relinquished his grip. He seeks to redeem our world one life, one soul, at a time. I am reminded of this every time I see Sasha.

As I write, our family vacations on the Gulf Coast. From my window, I look out on emerald waters as they gather into white foam and gently roll upon the shore, each day tearing down and sculpting anew the dunes into curious forms. Running through the surf is a girl. It is Sasha. She is laughing as her brothers test their skill on a small board and crash into the waves. Her skin is deeply tanned, and her hair, made blonder by the sun, is long and follows in her

Photo by Larry Alex Taunton

Sasha and her brothers. From left, Michael, Christopher, Sasha, and Zachary.

wake like a flame. Everything in her bearing emanates vitality and happiness. She is beautiful.

In the year that Sasha has been with us, she has grown seven inches taller and gained twenty pounds. Her HIV is well managed and her teeth are healthy. When she is not swimming, she is supposed to wear her glasses, though she often has to be reminded. She has forgotten most of her Russian and instead chatters away in an easy if heavily accented English.[3] She loves to shop, to play with Blitz, and to cook. A budding fashionista, she is quick to offer me advice on what I wear. Her faith is the simple and strong faith of a child. She enjoys stories from the Bible, and when she prays, she gives thanks to God for her family before all else.

In Sasha, Jesus Christ has made an answer to the wisdom

Photo by Christopher Taunton

Sasha with Blitz, at Lake Martin.

of our age. By redeeming her, he set forth a humble yet irre-
futable argument for the healing power of his touch. Sasha's
life, so graceless only a short time ago, is now a testament
to his grace. To those who have eyes to see and ears to hear,
Christ has sent Sasha into the world, bearing a message of
hope: the same redemptive power that he has so mercifully
displayed in her is on offer to entire nations. It says so in
his Word: "Blessed is the nation whose God is the LORD"
(Psalm 33:12).

The Debate Ends

The Judeo-Christian tradition has formed us in
the west; we are bound to it by ties which may
often be invisible, but which are there nonetheless.
It has formed the shape of our secularism; it has
formed even the shape of modern atheism.

—FLANNERY O'CONNOR IN *MYSTERY AND MANNERS*

ALMOST TWO YEARS AFTER OUR DISCUSSION IN THE RESTAURANT, Christopher Hitchens and I met again, this time at his Washington, D.C., apartment. His lovely wife, Carol, and his sweet daughter, Antonia, were gracious enough to host me for a pleasant breakfast before Hitch and I headed south on an eleven-hour road trip to Birmingham. Some five months after he was diagnosed with esophageal cancer, I was shocked by his appearance. Heavy doses of chemotherapy had left him emaciated and hairless, except for his eyelashes. His clothes hung off of him as though he were a boy wearing a man's garments. He was, nonetheless, looking forward to our journey, having packed a picnic lunch

223

and, predictably, enough Johnnie Walker for a battalion. And he had not forgotten my challenge.

"Have you a copy of Saint John with you?" Hitch asked with a smile. "If not, you know I *do* actually have one." With a wave of the hand, he pointed to his library.

"Not necessary." I was smiling, too. "I brought mine."

A few hours later we were winding our way through the Shenandoah Valley on a beautiful fall morning. As I drove, Hitch read aloud from the first chapter of John's gospel. For the next few hours, we discussed its meaning. When he referred to this discussion in a televised debate the next day, various media representatives asked me if we had argued. When I said that we had not, they lost interest. But that was the truth. It was a civilized, rational discussion. I did my best to move through the prologue of John's gospel verse by verse, and Christopher asked thoughtful questions. That's it.

The following month, however, was different. We met in public debate in Billings, Montana.[1] The theater marquee read "God or No God? A Debate—Christopher Hitchens vs. Larry Taunton." It was reminiscent of similar advertisements for heavyweight fights. Although we had debated one-on-one many times, this was our first *public* encounter.

The hall was full. Christopher, not I, was of course the real attraction. He was at the peak of his fame. His fans had traveled near and far to see him demolish another Christian. Such an outcome would serve to make them feel better about themselves and the philosophy of meaninglessness they had made their own.

Overall, the debate was a hard-fought but friendly affair. Perhaps the most critical moment of the contest came when

Photo by Christopher Taunton

The marquee for the debate.

we were arguing not over a point of history or philosophy, but over the nature of Christianity itself. One of the topics of discussion was "Are all religions the same?" I had three minutes before the moderator would cut me off. *What do I say?* I adopted a simple approach: rather than trying to explain all of the world's major religions and their distinguishing characteristics, I instead chose to speak of that Christian doctrine which separates Christianity from all other faiths: grace. Where other religions offer salvation via "to do" lists, Christianity alone among the world's great religions offers salvation through a Person who is accessed by the grace he so freely offers. Without grace, I argued, we are all without hope.

As I finished, the audience was utterly silent. Whether it was out of respect or bewilderment, I do not know. Whatever the reason, I am grateful for it. Too often, outsiders imagine Christianity to be a religion of self-righteous prigs who are slavishly obedient to the Law. Here was an opportunity to set the record straight, to proclaim the mercy of God as revealed in the person of Jesus Christ. Grace, properly articulated, has the effect of putting us all on the same level. Rather than speaking to you in condescending tones, I alert you to our common problem. *We*—you, me, the entire human race—are plagued by a fallen nature. What can save us from ourselves? *Grace!*

The debate over, I crossed the stage to shake Christopher's hand. "You were quite good tonight," he said with a charming smile as he accepted my proffered hand. "I think they enjoyed us."

"You were gentle with me," I said as we turned to walk off the stage.

He shook his head. "Oh, I held nothing back." He then surveyed the auditorium that still pulsed with energy. "We are still having dinner after the book signing?" he asked.

"Absolutely."

After a quick cigarette on the sidewalk near the back-stage door, he went back inside to meet his fans and sign their books. There was something macabre about it all. I had the unsettling feeling that these weren't people who cared about him in the least. Instead, they seemed like a bunch of groupies who wanted to have a photo taken with a famous but dying man so that one day they could show it to their atheist buddies and say, "I knew him before he died." It was a sad spectacle.

Turning away, I entered the foyer, where thirty or so Christians greeted me excitedly. Mostly students, they were encouraged by what had happened onstage that night. Someone had spoken for them, and it had put a bounce in their step. One young man told me that he had been close to abandoning his faith but that the debate had restored his confidence in the truth of the gospel. Another student said that she saw how she could use some of the same arguments. It is a daunting task, really, debating someone of Hitch's intellect and experience, but if this cheery gathering of believers thought I had done well, then all of the preparation and expense had been worth it.

An hour later, Hitch and I met my staff and family for dinner at a local steakhouse.

"Hello, Christopher Hitchens!" Sasha stood outside of the Montana Sky, awaiting our arrival excitedly. With her English still a work in progress, she assumed that the use of one's full name was the proper greeting.

"Good evening, young lady," he said. "Permit me to hold the door for you." Hitch grinned broadly.

"Thank you, Christopher Hitchens." Sasha, smiling ear to ear, skipped through the door.

The two had met before. "She's not what I had expected," Hitch had said to me at their introduction. This was a reference to Sasha's HIV. Lively and beautiful is not the mental image most have of someone with this condition.

At dinner, Christopher watched her from a nearby table. As Sasha laughed and talked to her brothers, her vivacious personality overflowing, Hitch looked amused, even touched. Sasha neither knew that she was being observed nor that she was a participant in a silent and undeclared debate. The contrast between these contestants was striking. Here he was, at sixty-something, an Oxonian, a best-selling author, and a celebrated public intellectual, while opposite him sat a poorly educated twelve-year-old girl who was still learning the basics of the English language. Even so, he was no match for her. *Sasha had been transformed by grace.*

Hitch has long maintained that he has never lost a debate. I would like to think that he had lost to me only a couple of hours earlier, that very night. But whatever the outcome of our contest, he had most certainly lost this silent, undeclared dinner debate to the most unlikely of champions. All of the clever theories contained in his books, lectures, and drawing room conversations seemed hollow before Sasha because the testimony of her life trumped any argument he could make against the gospel. But isn't that the grace effect? Working quietly, humbly, and animated by a Great Hope, it changes lives, even the lives of those who do not believe in it. Christopher smiled at her once more. *Yes*, I thought, *that is the grace effect indeed.*

Photo by Hannah Slamen

Sasha and the rest of the Taunton family at her brother Michael's wedding. Sasha was a bridesmaid.

Sasha catches the bouquet at her brother's wedding.

Sasha and her brothers.

Notes

Prologue

1. T. S. Eliot, *Christianity and Culture* (n.p.: Mariner Books, 1960), 200.
2. "The theme is an attempt to trace the defects of society back to the defects of human nature." *Lord of the Flies* (New York: Berkley, 1954), 204.

Chapter 1

1. Louis Berkhof, *Systematic Theology* (Grand Rapids: Wm. B. Eerdmans, 1976), 434.

Chapter 3

1. "Do Atheists Care Less?" *Maclean's* magazine online, May 6, 2010, http://www2.macleans.ca/2010/05/06/do-atheists-care-less/.
2. Christopher Hitchens, *The Portable Atheist: Essential Readings for the Nonbeliever*, 3rd ed. (Philadelphia: Da Capo Press, 2007), xiv.
3. Barna Group, "New Study Shows Trends in Tithing and Donating," April 14, 2008, http://www.barna.org/barna-update/article/18-congregations/41-new-study-shows-trends-in-tithing-and-donating?q=study+trend+tithing.

Chapter 4

1. An iPhone app.
2. https://www.osac.gov/Reports/report.cfm?contentID=113936. No longer accessible.

Notes

Chapter 5

1. Mark Rachkevych, "Ukraine's Richest Zoom Ahead of Rest of Nation," *Kyiv Post*, June 24, 2008; available on the website of Ocnus.net, at: http://www.ocnus.net/artman2/publish/ Business_1/Ukraine_s_Richest_Zoom_Ahead_of_Rest_of_ Nation_printer.shtml.

Chapter 6

1. Daniel Fisher, "The Most Corrupt Countries: Who Tops the List? A Nation So Bad Piracy Is Considered a Legitimate Trade," *Forbes*, November 1, 2010, http://www.forbes.com/2010/11/01/most -currupt-countries-2010-business-beltway-currupt-countries.html.
2. Corruption Perceptions Index 2010 Results, Transparency International, http://www.transparency.org/policy_research/ surveys_indices/cpi/2010/results.

Chapter 8

1. John F. Kennedy, remarks in Naples, Italy, at NATO Headquarters, July 2, in *Public Papers of the Presidents of the United States, John F. Kennedy, 1963, January 1 to November 22, 1963* (USGPO, 1964).
2. *The State and Revolution*, reprint of the English translation of the *Selected Works of V. I. Lenin*, vol. 2 (Whitefish, MT: Kessinger Publishing, 2004), 100.
3. Developed by Dr. Laurence J. Peter in the 1960s, the Peter Principle is the theory that members of a given business, government, or organization are often promoted one level beyond their competence.
4. Fyodor Dostoevsky, *The Brothers Karamazov*, trans. Constance Garnett (New York: Modern Library, 1996), 26.
5. Brezhnev once defined Soviet society as "a society where a scientific and materialistic concept of the world dominates." [See Mikhail Geller, *Utopia in Power* (New York: Simon & Schuster, 1992), 673.]
6. Francis Schaeffer, *How Should We Then Live?* (Wheaton, IL: Crossway, 1983), 26.

7. Alexis de Tocqueville and Reeve Henry, *Democracy in America*, vol. 2 (n.p.: BiblioBazaar, 2008), 738.
8. Sergei Iuelevich Vitte, *The Memoirs of Count Sergei Witte*, trans. Sidney Harcave (New York: M. E. Sharpe, 1990), 413.
9. Sheila Fitzpatrick, *The Russian Revolution* (New York: Oxford University Press, 2008), 8–9.

Chapter 9

1. Aldous Huxley, *Brave New World*, Library Binding ed. (Cutchogue, NY: Buccaneer Books, 1991), 99.
2. Alan Ball, "State Children: Soviet Russia's Besprizornye and the New Socialist Generation," *Russian Review* 52, no. 2 (April 1993): 229.
3. Ibid.
4. Ibid., 234.
5. Ibid., 246.
6. Ibid., 244.
7. Sheila Fitzpatrick, *The Commissariat of Enlightenment: Soviet Organization of Education and the Arts Under Lunacharsky* (Cambridge, UK: Cambridge University Press, 1970), 30.
8. A. S. Makarenko, A. S. Makarenko Reference Archive: Lectures to Parents: Lecture 1, Marxist.org, "General Conditions for Bringing Up a Family," http://www.marxists.org/reference/archive/makarenko/works/lectures/lec01.html.
9. Geller, *Utopia in Power*, 286.
10. Kathleen Hunt, *Abandoned to the State: Cruelty and Neglect in Russian Orphanages* (n.p.: Human Rights Watch, 1998), 28.
11. "Rise and Demise of Orphanages in Ukraine," *European Journal of Social Work* (online publication date April 1, 2003): 61.
12. Ibid., 57.
13. Mark R. Elliott, "Russians at Risk," *Religion in Eastern Europe* 28, no. 3 (August 2008), available online at http://www.georgefox.edu/academics/undergrad/departments/soc-swk/ree/Elliott_Russian_Aug%202008.pdf (see p. 9 of PDF).
14. Hunt, *Abandoned to the State*, 28.
15. "While UNICEF acknowledges that many of these children are at

increased risk from their underlying conditions, it attributes part of the high mortality figures to crowding, poor hygiene, and low standards of care" (ibid., 27).

16. Boris Pasternak, *Doctor Zhivago*, transs. Manya Harari and Max Hayward (New York: Everyman's Library, Alfred A. Knopf, 1991), 449.

Chapter 11

1. Dostoevsky, *The Brothers Karamazov*, 312.
2. Anna Reid, *Borderland: A Journey Through the History of Ukraine* (Boulder, CO: Westview Press, 1999, 2000), 194.
3. http://travel.state.gov/adopt.html (2009). No longer accessible.

Chapter 12

1. Victor Hugo, *Les Misérables* (New York: Simon & Schuster, 2005), 542.
2. See Associated Press, "Ukraine's Ex-PM Criticizes Dress Code," October 6, 2010, http://abcnews.go.com/Health/wireStory?id=11812705.

Chapter 14

1. Don Felder, Glenn Frey, and Don Henley, "Hotel California," prod. Bill Szymczyk, Asylum Records, 1977, 45 rpm.

Chapter 15

1. Andrew Cook, *Ace of Spies: The True Story of Sidney Reilly* (n.p.: Tempus Publishing, 2004), 238.
2. Jimmy Page and Robert Plant, "The Immigrant Song," prod. Jimmy Page, Atlantic Records, 1970, 45 rpm.

Chapter 16

1. *Wikipedia*, s.v. "Yuri Gagarin," http://en.wikipedia.org/wiki/Yuri_Gagarin.

2. C. S. Lewis, *A Mind Awake: An Anthology of C. S. Lewis* (New York: Harcourt Brace Jovanovich, 1980), 74. Also in Lewis, *The Seeing Eye and Other Selected Essays from* Christian Reflections, ed. Walter Hooper (New York: Ballantine, 1986), 230.
3. Richard Dawkins, *The God Delusion*, 1st Am. Ed. (New York: Houghton-Mifflin Harcourt, 2006), 218–19.
4. Olivera Petrovich, e-mail message to and conversation with author, January 2011.

Chapter 20

1. Harriet Beecher Stowe, *Uncle Tom's Cabin*, ed. William Frost (n.p.: ZetaCraft Publishing, 2010), 395.
2. Ruth Gledhill, "Scandal and Schism Leave Christians Praying for a 'New Reformation,'" *Times* (UK), April 2, 2010, http://www .timesonline.co.uk/tol/comment/faith/article7085129.ece.
3. Adoption experts will tell you that the loss of a child's native language is common and should not be a source of anxiety. It is, they say, easily recovered. Since memories, often bad memories, are associated with language, this is not altogether regrettable.

Epilogue

1. Titled "God or No God?" this debate is available on the Fixed Point Foundation website along with a group study guide.

About the Author

LARRY ALEX TAUNTON IS FOUNDER AND EXECUTIVE DIRECTOR of Fixed Point Foundation, an initiative dedicated to defending and promoting Christianity in the public square. In that role, he has engaged some of the most vociferous critics of the Christian faith.

In addition to producing several Fixed Point films, Larry, along with his team, launched LookUp316.com in February 2011, a project that put the hopeful message of John 3:16 before a Super Bowl audience. He has been a frequent guest on a variety of television and radio shows, and has been quoted by the *New York Times*, *USA Today*, the *Daily Mail*, *Atlantic*, and *Vanity Fair*, among many other newspapers and magazines. When not writing, teaching, or producing, Larry travels widely, speaking on issues of faith and culture. He and his wife, Lauri, have four children and live in Birmingham, Alabama.

Acknowledgments

AUTHORS WILL TELL YOU THAT WRITING A BOOK IS TEDIOUS business. "Between the idea and the reality lies the shadow," T. S. Eliot observed. Eliot knew a thing or two about writing books. Over the last year or so, I have discovered a few of them, and certainly one is that the shadow between the idea for a book and the reality of it grows very long indeed. In my journey, there were many people who continually encouraged me in this endeavor. Chief among them were my wife, Lauri; our children, Christopher, Zachary, and Michael; and my mom, Judith. They sat and listened intently to me as I read portions of the manuscript to them and solicited their feedback. They contributed ideas and corrected details of the narrative.

But there were many others. Shara Haden read my blogs about our experiences and insisted that I turn them into a book. Professor John Lennox urged me to write while the emotional power of the story was still fresh in my mind. Pastor Andrew Siegenthaler and Bill Wortman helped me think through the theological aspects of the concept, while Dr. David Schroeder tested the historical accuracy of my thesis. My assistant, Mary Laura Rogan, provided invaluable aid in proofing and correcting the manuscript while fetching coffee and sweet tea. Mike Murphy read the book and, believing in its potential, immediately took it to publishers. One of the first to read it was Joel Miller of Thomas Nelson. An accomplished author in his own right, Joel agreed with Mike's assessment of the book and pursued it patiently. Thanks also to the remaining staff and board of Fixed Point Foundation for lending me their professional expertise and permitting me the time to write the book: Ed Haden, Alan Halbrooks, Ben Halbrooks, Woody Jacobs, George Jones, Alex Leath, Dan McCrary, Rebekah Page, Dr. Steve Skinner, Will Hill Tankersley, Jay Weatherly, and Rob Williamson. And to my editors, Kristen Parrish and Judith Pierson, whose guidance was consistent and their editing pens gentle—thank you.

And I would especially like to thank Jana Lombardo of Lifeline Adoption. This agency was the only one we could find that was willing to help us adopt an HIV-positive child. Together we navigated the process and opened the way to more adoptions of children with this disease.

Most of all, however, there is my inspiration for this book: my daughter, Sasha "Alex" Taunton, a young lady of indomitable spirit and courage. If a man of my age is permitted to have heroes, she is mine. May the story of her triumph through grace given and grace received serve to inspire many beyond those who have been privileged to know her.

Mary's Needleart Supplies & Framing of Rt. 11 S., Sandy Creek

315-387-5903

Hours: Tues. & Thurs. 10:00 to 5:00; Sat. 10:00 to 3:00

> Open any day with the letter "T" in it! <

www.marysneedleart.com

Lizzie★Kate

TRUNK SHOW

Thru Sat., July 21, 2012

Whimsical, cutesy, (they'll make you smile!)

"Snippets", "Flip-its", "Double Flips", "Quick-its", "Boxers", Charts
Kits, Punchneedle Kits, Embellishments - Buttons, Charms and More
Even if you don't cross stitch, you'll be happy you stopped by.
Who knows, you might be inspired to start!

27TH ANNUAL CHRISTMAS-IN-JULY

July 17 - July 31

25% OFF all in-stock Christmas merchandise

(Only about 5 months until Christmas!!!)

USA 32

ALOHA

YRACUSE NY
PM
03 JUL 2012

MARY'S NEEDLEART SUPPLIES & FRAMING
OF RT. 11 S., SANDY CREEK
240 MILLER RD
LACONA NY 13083-3144

ADDRESS SERVICE REQUESTED

FRANCIS J & LIZ W MAUNDER
2054 CO RT 26
PARISH, NY 13131

The Grace Effect
Discussion Guide

I. The Debate Begins (preface and prologue)

There have been innumerable debates about God's existence, the credibility of the Gospel accounts, and so on. These are important issues. But the question here is the most practical of all: What kind of society do we want to live in? Is it preferable to live in a society primarily influenced by a Judeo-Christian worldview or in one that is atheistic in nature? This section presents the relevant arguments offered at a late-night gathering of seasoned—but friendly—combatants who disagree on this question.

1. It may seem surprising that these men went to dinner after an intense public debate. How do you think a friendship between an atheist and a Christian could be of mutual benefit? Do you think it is a true friendship? Why or why not?

2. Hitchens believes that "man is unquestionably evil." Do you agree? If so, how do you define "evil"?

3. Taunton and Lennox draw a distinction between the conduct of self-professed Christians and the actual teachings of Christ as recorded in the Gospels. Is this differentiation a sufficient defense against Hitchens's criticisms of the behavior of the Russian Orthodox Church and televangelists? Why or why not?

4. Is it your perception that, as Taunton insists, the civil rights movement is an "example of evil defeated by a people who were motivated by a Christian conscience"?

5. On the whole, do you think Christianity is a force for good or evil in modern society? Why?

RECOMMENDED READING: *God Is Not Great*, Christopher Hitchens; *Has Science Buried God*? John Lennox

RECOMMENDED VIEWING: *Is God Great*? A debate between Christopher Hitchens and John Lennox (available on the Fixed Point Foundation website: www.fixed-point.org)

II. An Atheistic Society Is Without (Much) Grace (chaps. 1–3)

This part of the book describes the Christian concept of common grace and how it informs our cultural attitudes.

According to Taunton, this "grace effect" is an observable phenomenon—life is demonstrably better where authentic Christianity flourishes. This section records the expectations and first impressions the Tauntons had when they arrived in Ukraine. That Ukraine is culturally different from America is not relevant to the debate. All cultures differ in ways that have no significant implications: Americans drive on the right side of the road; British, on the left. Very well. But the contrasts emphasized here reveal moral standards of fairness and compassion. Many of the Ukrainian expectations and attitudes show how little common grace has influenced their government.

1. What are some encouraging signs of common grace in the first experience the Tauntons have in Kiev? Which convey a *lack* of common grace?
2. What factors do you think account for why atheists give significantly less to nonprofits than Christians do?
3. It is clear that Ukrainians tolerate and incubate many cultural norms that subvert the sanctity of life. In what major areas of the culture do Americans tolerate and incubate the devaluing of human life?

RECOMMENDED READING: *The Devil's Delusion*, David Berlinski

RECOMMENDED VIEWING: *Can Atheism Save Europe*? A debate between Christopher Hitchens and John Lennox at the Edinburgh International Festival (available on the Fixed Point Foundation website: www.fixed-point.org)

III. How an Atheistic Society Suppresses Grace (chaps. 4–7)

In these chapters, the author argues that Ukraine's government institutions impede grace. As a result, its positive force does not stream through the legal, economic, and political machinery of that government. The entire population is ordered and regulated by less humane standards than those to which Americans are accustomed. What is the primary cause of this difference? It isn't that Americans are better people. Rather, the Russian Orthodox Church was drained of grace centuries ago. The rejection of *biblical* Christianity in times past crippled the nation's future.

1. Ukrainian attitudes toward the law seem, for the most part, in striking contrast to American attitudes. Why do you think this is so?
2. Why is an economic system alone—whether socialistic or capitalistic—insufficient to develop and sustain economic fairness?
3. Explain why the author thinks "the devil is a bureaucrat."

4. In practical terms, how can common grace slowly improve Ukraine's "corruption index" of 134th out of 180 countries?

5. What were the practical consequences of Prince Vladimir's choice of Greek Orthodoxy over Roman Christianity, Islam, and Judaism?

RECOMMENDED READING: *The World Turned Upside Down*, Melanie Phillips; *The Brothers Karamazov*, Fyodor Dostoevsky

IV. Atheists in Charge (chaps. 8–9)

In the debate over whether a society is better served by atheism or Christianity, atheists point to *theoretical* models instead of real examples (like China, North Korea, the former Soviet Union, etc.). In this section, the author defines socialism as antithetical to Christianity and then walks us through history to show how this is so. He then demonstrates to us how the "orphanage archipelago" represents a poignant example of what a world created by atheists looks like.

1. Define "communism" and "socialism" and explain why the author thinks that these economic and political theories hinge upon *spiritual* issues.

2. Is Christianity primarily about meeting physical needs? Why or why not?

3. What is your response to the following statement of Richard Dawkins: "Suppose there is no hope. Suppose there is no justice. Suppose there's nothing but misery and darkness and bleakness. Suppose there's nothing that we would wish for, nothing that we would hope for. Too bad!"?

4. Do you agree with George Washington's statement in his farewell address: "Reason and experience both forbid us to expect that national morality can prevail in exclusion of religious principle"? Why or why not?

5. What were the major assumptions about human existence that influenced the creation of the orphanage system under Lunacharsky and Makarenko? How does Christianity differ with regard to these major assumptions?

RECOMMENDED READING: *A Peoples' Tragedy*, Orlando Figes; *Brave New World*, Aldous Huxley

V. Divine Creation and the Value of a Soul (chaps. 10–12)

It is the nature of secular societies to devalue human life. As a former communist country, this attitude persists in Ukraine. By contrast, common grace, flowing as it does out of a Christian worldview, elevates human life, regarding it as the pinnacle of God's creation.

1. How does one best measure whether a given society elevates or degrades the sanctity of life?
2. Does Zachary's experience at McDonald's represent a neutral cultural difference or a deeper phenomenon that relates to common grace? Why?
3. It is clear that the author grew impatient and even angry through his experience. Indeed, he quotes a passage in Exodus in which God is said to be "angry." Can some forms of anger be a virtue? If so, how?
4. Do you think Americans are more compassionate solely because of the tradition of economic prosperity or because of other factors too?

RECOMMENDED READING: *Borderland*, Anna Reid

VI. Facing Challenges Resulting from Grace (chaps. 13–14)

It is a common misconception that Christian grace offers a kind of blank check to people, as if grace exempts them from any sense of responsibility. In these chapters the author relates some new challenges Sasha faces as a direct consequence of the grace shown to her. These would never have arisen had she not been delivered from her life in the orphanage system. In overcoming these challenges, faith proved to be essential. She had to muster the confident persistence to accomplish things previously unknown to her.

The Grace Effect Discussion Guide

But she also needed to know that, while she might doubt herself, others truly believed in her.

1. Sasha faces greater challenges in her education than the average American student. Describe how common grace as exhibited through the gift of parents is critical to a child's education and development.
2. How was the author's handling of Sasha's refusal to work on the alphabet an example of grace?
3. Does "believing in a student" mean that we should encourage him/her to aim at whatever his/her "dreams" are? Why or why not?
4. How does Sasha's newly discovered "freedom" differ from the typical American's notions of "freedom"?

RECOMMENDED READING: *The Art of Teaching*, Gilbert Highet

VII. The Foundations of a New Life (chaps. 15–17)

This section draws our attention to the ground level of life and the human experience: family and community. No one is born into this world without a history and an identity. An orphan faces the unique challenge of knowing very little about his or her family history even while being deeply shaped by that history. As we mature, we enter into a larger community of family, friends, and acquaintances that can be strongly positive or negative. According to Taunton, the force with the greatest potential to create good families and communities is grace. Even so, that is not the primary purpose of common grace. Common grace is meant to give people a foretaste of *heavenly* grace. It is meant to cultivate a desire to enjoy an eternal home with God.

1. Communists sought to suppress their true history and invent a new one. Why?
2. Are there negative consequences for societies or individuals when they do not know their real histories?
3. How has your life been shaped by your forebears?
4. What are the implications of Dr. Olivera Petrovich's research? In what ways does her research confirm teachings in the Bible?
5. Do you think Sasha's experience with prayer is compelling? Why or why not?
6. Sasha's HIV proved a concern for the Tauntons, not just medically but also socially. They wondered how she would be received in their community of relationships. Do you think American Christians are good examples of common grace in respect to this infirmity? Cite examples from your experience.

VIII. Grace Given Becomes Grace Received (chaps. 18–19)

A temptation for all parents who adopt a child is to see themselves as the primary dispensers of grace. After all, they don't *have* to pay large sums of money, carve out huge chunks of time, and make innumerable daily sacrifices to welcome and accommodate an orphan. They have chosen to do so out of a deep compassion and kindness. But as we learn in this climactic part of the book, grace given becomes grace received. The Tauntons gave an incalculable gift of a new life to Sasha. That is obvious. What may not be so easily seen is that Sasha is a gift to them.

1. The Tauntons' interaction with American (and French) government administrators was markedly different from what they had experienced with Ukrainian officials. How were these expressions of kindness related to common grace?
2. The author says that Sasha's first interactions with American culture resulted in some comedic episodes. What factors shape the rules that govern how we interact as a society? How are they influenced by common grace—or how do they run counter to it?
3. Describe the practical ways in which Christianity's influence directly benefited Sasha in her first weeks in America.
4. Who around you might be sending his or her

"flare high into a night sky"? What can you do to show common grace to that person (or people)?

IX. A Debate Ends: How One Life Refutes Atheism and Gives Hope to Entire Nations (chap. 20 and epilogue)

The question up for debate in this book has not been whether Christianity was a positive force in the formation of Western civilization. Even Hitchens cedes this in the late-night conversation recounted in the prologue. The more important question is whether Christianity should continue to be a primary influence in Western society. Is Christianity an *inherently* positive force in the formation, development, and maintenance of society? Taunton's argument is that the life and experience of this one little girl proves that the answer is yes.

1. What does the author mean when he says, "Only a Christian culture could produce a Richard Dawkins"?
2. Given that Richard Dawkins has argued for many years that belief in God is "delusional" and "very, very dangerous," why do you think he now says, "Christianity might be a bulwark against something worse"?
3. Do you think the author is right when he says that there has never been a Christian nation? Why or why not?

4. Both Sasha and Hitchens suffer from life-threatening illnesses. At a practical level, what does Christianity offer someone in these circumstances? At a practical level, what does Christianity offer someone in these circumstances? What does atheism offer?

5. Do you agree with the author that Sasha's experience validates the conclusion that Christianity should be a primary influence in society? Why or why not?

RECOMMENDED READING: *The Closing of the American Mind*, Allan Bloom; *What's So Great About Christianity*, Dinesh D'Souza

RECOMMENDED VIEWING: *God or No God?* A debate between Christopher Hitchens and Larry Taunton (available on the Fixed Point Foundation website: www.fixed-point.org)